Marshall & Mehrtens

A Season of Two Halves

Marshall & Mehrtens

A Season of Two Halves

with Phil Gifford

Hodder Moa Beckett

ISBN 1-86958-799-5

© 2001 – original text Justin Marshall and Andrew Mehrtens
The moral rights of the authors have been asserted

© 2001 – design and format Hodder Moa Beckett Publishers Ltd

Published in 2001 by Hodder Moa Beckett Publishers Limited
[a member of the Hodder Headline Group]
4 Whetu Place, Mairangi Bay, Auckland, New Zealand

Designed and produced by Hodder Moa Beckett Publishers Limited
Written by Phil Gifford

Printed by Publishing Press Ltd, Auckland

ABOUT THE WRITER

Phil Gifford has been writing about rugby since 1965, and is currently the co-host of the More FM breakfast show in Christchurch, judged the best in New Zealand at the 2000 national radio awards. He has written four rugby biographies, and invented the satirical rugby character, 'Loosehead Len'. He lives in Christchurch with his wife, Jan.

ACKNOWLEDGEMENTS

The writers and publishers would like to thank Peter Bush, Photosport and, of course, Justin and Mehrts for the photographs which appear throughout this book.

Contents

Introduction

The former Australian prop Chris Handy once said that it was no use asking him how a game of rugby had gone.

'I'm a prop,' said Buddha, named for the physical resemblance. 'I see the whole game out of me bum.'

By contrast, who better to take us behind the scenes with Canterbury, the Crusaders and the All Blacks than Justin Marshall and Andrew Mehrtens?

When it comes to players with the most opinions on the game, on referees, on training, on fitness, on life, and on the rules of euchre, you can't go past halfbacks and first-fives.

It takes a lot to slow down the men just behind the pack, and the only recorded case involves Grizz Wyllie, in the days when he was a fierce captain and No 8 for Canterbury in the 1970s.

After picking up the ball at the base of the scrum for the first 30 minutes of one provincial game, his inside backs, Lyn Davis and Doug Bruce, demanded they be allowed the ball.

Wyllie relented, the ball spun through the red and black backline, but was then spilled by the centre. 'That's it,' barked Wyllie. 'You pricks have had your chance for the day.'

Nevertheless, it's hard to imagine even Wyllie being able to repress Justin and Mehrts.

Coaches have commented on the free spirit that runs through them both. Vance Stewart, their first Canterbury coach, claimed that if there were two options available in a game during Mehrts' early years in the Canterbury team then Mehrts would always take the more difficult one, just for the challenge.

Individually they're very different rugby players. Justin's hugely physical, hard as nails, and thrives on contact. Mehrts is elusive, the reader of the game.

But there are large areas where their rugby converges too, most notably in a fierce competitiveness that drives both of them. If that edge seems easier to read in the way Justin plays rugby, check out the story in this book on Mehrts and the game with a football in a hotel car park.

And what they totally have in common is a sense of humour that doesn't get under anyone's skin because the butt of a lot of the jokes is themselves.

They've never taken themselves too seriously. Mehrts mocks his own lack of washboard abs. Justin reckons that some of the Mehrtens humour is way too difficult for someone like himself who hasn't been to university.

It was Justin who frankly admitted that when he was given his first All Black test jersey in France in 1995 he took it back to his hotel room and 'stared at it for ages wondering if I was man enough to put it on'.

The nearest you'll get to either of the pair boasting is when they talk of their work on the All Black laundry committee. There they don't hesitate to suggest they set a benchmark that others in the rugby soap powder brigade will struggle to better.

There have been players in the past who have combined well on the rugby field without being especially close friends, but it seems more than a coincidence that these two are good mates as well as teaming up so smoothly on the paddock.

You'll find some serious thoughts in this book, and hopefully a lot of humour. If you happen to draw the conclusion by the last page that Justin and Mehrts are good jokers, you'd be absolutely right.

Phil Gifford
Christchurch, 2000

Konnichiwa, Bonjour, Ciao!

In the past, All Black tours to Europe have lasted as long as six months, with boat trips, formal dinner after formal dinner, and almost 40 matches being played in all. At the start of the 21st century the All Blacks' trip to Japan, France and Italy ran at a different speed but, as Justin and Mehrts reveal in this tour diary, some things never change. There are high points, low points, sombre moments and, thankfully, plenty of humour.

Friday October 27 to Sunday October 29, 2000. Takapuna, Auckland.

Both: The Poenamo Hotel was where we both assembled when we were first together in the All Blacks in 1995.

It had been a traditional meeting place for the All Blacks for quite a few years, and then we steered away from it. It was good to get back there actually.

They've done the hotel up while we've been away and done that quite nicely, too.

Mehrts: I did start to think that I was the curse of the 'Poe', because the last time we went to France and Italy I was roomed with Josh Kronfeld, who subsequently got injured and missed the tests over there.

This time when I got to Auckland I'd heard the rumours that Craig Dowd had injured his back. I found myself in a room on my own, so I figured I'd initially been with Craig.

But then, not only had I 'worked' Craig without him even being there, Carl Hoeft turned up as my room-mate, and then proceeded to blow his calf out. So I was back to my old tricks as the jinx. Luckily, Gordon Slater didn't join the tour until we got to Europe.

We had the same old jokes at the start of the tour about Christmas coming early when the gear was dished out. The general rule is that you don't turn up with anything except your underpants and a toothbrush.

Justin: We trained across the road at the Takapuna Rugby Club, which is very handy, and a helluva lot better than hopping on a bus all the time, especially when you're training twice a day as we were at that stage.

Mehrts: I have to disgaree. Training being so close means there's no nice 25 to 30 minute bus trip for that final bit of sleep before training. You're into it straight away.

Monday, October 30. To Japan.

Both: We flew to Japan, to Narita, and then went by bus to the Nippon Aerobics Centre, a resort complex near Chiba where we trained for a couple of nights before we went to Tokyo.

Mehrts: The first thing that struck all of us from the time we arrived at the airport, to the bus, to the hotel, was how clean and immaculately presented everything was.

There was no rubbish anywhere and everything was modern and efficient.

Justin: It was the first time I'd been to Japan, which was a bit of an eye opener. The hotels we stayed at were very good and the people looked after us really well.

But for some reason, though, they felt they had to cook us

western food. It's a bit like when we're in Italy – they gave us skinless chicken, like we eat in camp in New Zealand.

It doesn't seem to make any sense really. We were looking to tuck into some good Japanese food. The first night we were there we got it and we thought it'd be great.

The big boys up front were a bit disappointed they couldn't get into that good teppan and the deep fried stuff. But the Japanese cooks followed the rules pretty stringently, and most of the food was per the plan.

We found the rooms reasonably interesting. Some of the big boys were rumbling into rooms with tiny wee baths and showers, tiny wee beds with what felt like rocks for pillows, and slippers at the door.

Mehrts: Everything was quite small. **For some of the bigger guys it must have been a bit like living in a dolls' house. Being the size I am, I was fine.**

The beds were right down on the floor, with futons and pillows that were pretty unusual for us. The lower pillow was actually stone or rock, with a pillow on top that had buckwheat in it.

Naturally the talk in the morning was that the top pillow was for a midnight snack. The pillow absorbed the dribble in the night, and in the morning you had a sack of wheat to eat.

The other very obvious difference in the hotel was that there wasn't a single television channel that was in English. There were about six channels, but they were all Japanese speaking.

Straight away we went to guys like Christian Cullen, saying, 'What the hell are you going to do for three days?' There were little rooms, with little beds and no English on TV.

We felt for some of those faster guys. They rely pretty heavily on their beds and TVs when they're on tour. They get into a hotel and wrap themselves up in bed and either sleep or watch telly. I don't know if it's energy conservation, or what it is, but it does seem to work for them.

The speedy guys in the Crusaders like Marika Vunibaka and Afato So'oalo are like that, and so is Christian Cullen. I'm starting to wonder if I should sleep a lot more during the week, and then maybe I'd get quicker.

Justin: A few of the taller boys looked a little ridiculous in the robes they supplied. **They were very short, which meant that someone like Norm Maxwell looked as if he was in a big white T-shirt with his slippers on.**

Mehrts: I was walking around looking a picture in those robes, not to mention the wee leather slip-ons, too. After a long flight you do feel a bit sweaty, which I hate, so I get out of the travelling gear as quickly as possible.

Both: Before the game we moved into Tokyo to the Hilton Hotel to get ready for the match with the Pacific Barbarians, who were almost all New Zealanders, most of them guys who have been playing in Japan.

There were a lot of guys we knew in the Barbarians – Arran Pene, Graeme Bachop, Jamie Joseph, Ant Strachan and Liam Barry, who had been on the trip in 1995 to France and Italy. We pretty much knew everyone there, which was really good.

Justin: It was good to catch up with them after the game, to find out what their views were on rugby, now that they've been living in a different culture, basically being over there trying to secure a future.

Mehrts: We had a chance on the day before the game to have a small wander around Tokyo, which we found reasonably expensive.

Five of us wandered into Starbucks. I foolishly offered to buy a round, which cost about $NZ60, for five coffees. To be fair, the coffee was really good. It wouldn't have been so well spent if the coffee had been bad.

The only thing about Japan that I found wasn't terribly immaculate was that so many people are smokers.

As it happens, the New Zealand union called this the Friendship Tour, but it could just as easily have been called the Smoking Tour, because we hit three of the biggest smoking spots in the world – Japan, France and Italy. Just massive amounts of smoking going on.

Friday, November 3.

The All Blacks beat the Pacific Barbarians 50-10 at Prince Chichibu Stadium, Tokyo.

For the All Blacks: Tries by Bruce Reihana (2), Carlos Spencer, Pita Alatini, Doug Howlett, Daryl Gibson and Justin Marshall; one penalty goal and four conversions by Andrew Mehrtens; two conversions by Carlos Spencer.

For the Pacific Barbarians: Try by Graeme Bachop; penalty goal and conversion by Andy Miller.

Justin: Mehrts and I played the second half, which was probably quite fortunate for us because the Barbarians were all fire and brimstone in the first half, but started to get a bit of fatigue in the second half when we were able to run away with it a bit.

Mehrts: We did escape the fury in the first 40 minutes, although the Barbarians did us a lot of good by giving us a really good run.

They'd had a hell of a celebration getting together, because although there are big numbers of Kiwis up there, I don't think they get the chance to physically get together a lot.

Guys like Jamie Joseph, Arran Pene and Blair Larsen pumped it up and really ran hard into it. Some of the things those guys have got in their rugby means it doesn't matter how long they've been playing or where they're playing – it all comes naturally. The mental toughness and the hunger to succeed stays there and can be called on whenever it's needed.

Justin: It was interesting hearing how much they'd been looking forward to the game, and how weird a feeling it was to stand on the opposite side of the haka.

A lot of them had done the haka before, as All Blacks, but to stand on the other side and face it, knowing that was what they used to do, was certainly different. I can honestly say that I don't know what it would be like either.

After the game I was talking to Matt Sexton and he said it was just awesome to watch, that it felt quite intimidating, and he felt privileged to be facing it.

They were fired up for the game and there were some good players there. Andy Miller and Phillipe Rayasi had played with us in the Crusaders way back in 1996 . . . it's hard to keep up with who is playing where outside New Zealand these days.

I was quite taken aback by the number of New Zealanders in Japan. There were guys I didn't even realise were over there, or were still playing rugby at that level.

Mehrts: I was quite rapt, because I was able to swap a jersey with the 'Emperor', Willie Lose (the former Auckland and North Harbour loose forward). He's a guy that for a while was e-mailing me from Japan.

When he was in New Zealand his nickname was the 'Prince', but when he got to Japan they had trouble pronouncing it, so he became the Emperor. That was his e-mail address, *theemperor@* **wherever he was.** Willie's got a bit of a cult following in New Zealand rugby, because he's such a hard case.

I said to him, when we swapped jerseys, that mine might be too tight for him, but then I remembered that wearing really tight clothes was right up his alley, so he probably wanted one my size anyway.

Both: After the game there was a brief aftermatch, which was reasonably relaxed. It gave us the chance to have a drink and a yarn with some of the guys we knew in the Barbarians.

Mehrts: I had the chance to catch up with a number of the Barbarians in a bar down the street after the game and it was encouraging to see that not a lot changes.

When I walked in Richard Turner was up dancing on a table, and before long Ant Strachan had his shirt off. Graeme Bachop was in a corner sipping away quietly, with a wee smile on his face, taking it all in. That was really good.

PETER BUSH

Dave Gallaher's grave at Poperhinge.

Saturday, November 4. To France.

Both: The next morning we had a very early start on the bus. That was followed by an internal flight before we headed off to France. After arriving in France we had a train trip to our hotel in Lille, the Alliance Couvent Des Minimes. In all it was about 20 hours of travel.

We came into Paris on the Saturday morning, with our body clocks a little out of kilter. Then we had to organise what gear we wanted to go on a truck straight down to Lille.

Mehrts: We took the TGV to Lille, the superfast train, and I loved that. **We were shot up to Lille at speeds of up to 240km/h. I really enjoy the train systems in Europe.**

As it happens, the Italian train system is even more efficient than the French system, and some years ago, when I played in Italy, I loved going by train everywhere.

Justin: The point of going to Lille was that the test with

17

Toddy Blackadder lays a specially bred rose, called 'Lest We Forget', at Dave Gallaher's grave at the Nine Elms Cemetery. With Toddy is All Black manager Andrew Martin.

France, on Armistice Day, was for the Dave Gallaher Trophy, named after the captain of the 1905 All Blacks who toured Britain and France.

He died of wounds received in the Battle of Passchendaele in 1917, and we were joined by the players from the New Zealand A team. Together we paid a visit to the war graves, at Poperhinge where Dave Gallaher and so many New Zealanders are buried.

It was an incredibly humbling experience to go to the graves, which were sited on what was once a base for wounded soldiers during the war.

We saw the graves and the memorial there, and then went to the actual site of the Battle of Passchendaele.

We also went to the town of Le Quesnoy where the New Zealand soldiers climbed the ancient walls of the town in

November 1918, to liberate it, rather than bombarding it to pieces.

Mehrts: It was awe inspiring, to really think of what it was like for the soldiers to be going to a foreign land and be fighting with and for strangers.

Le Quesnoy was a fortified town and the Germans were inside the walls, but so were all the people of the town. Nobody had been evacuated.

There were machinegun nests all around the town and it was a matter of finding a small gap, scaling walls and gradually taking control of the town. The Kiwis were able to get in there and were helped out by the townfolk once they got inside.

We like to think of ourselves as having a bit of Kiwi ingenuity, with a go get 'em spirit, and it was a real boost to our patriotism to hear what had happened in Le Quesnoy. There still seems to be a certain affinity between the people in the town and the New Zealanders.

Justin: The good thing was that we had two New Zealand military historians, Chris Pugsley and Ian McGibbon, to explain to us what the soldiers had to go through; how they had to crawl through mud, slept in muddy trenches, were trapped in barbed wire, and generally what they suffered through the whole campaign.

It was quite humbling, because where we went was where the New Zealanders had two of their finest moments in World War I.

I thought it was great that we actually went to see what the whole thing was about. We could have played a test for the Dave Gallaher Trophy, but people my age and younger wouldn't actually know what you were playing for.

But once we knew that the man was a real hero, as were all the New Zealanders who were there, it gave some real meaning to the trophy.

The French are very passionate about it and know the details of what happened, so it was important that we did, too.

It sunk in for everyone in the team, that the New Zealanders who went to Europe then had been fighting for their country. I know that personally I drew a lot of courage from what I saw.

Those men faced death, and a lot died for their country. I know it made me feel proud to be a New Zealander.

Saturday, November 11.

The All Blacks beat France 39–26 at the Stade de France, Paris.
For the All Blacks: Tries by Christian Cullen and Doug Howlett; nine penalty goals and a conversion by Andrew Mehrtens.
For France: Tries by Philippe Bernat-Salles and Fabien Pelous: four penalty goals and two conversions by Christophe Lamaison.

Both: We knew that on Armistice Day the French had a great record against the All Blacks, and knew we'd face a huge effort from the French.

We were as passionate as them to win the game and, playing at the brand new stadium, with a sellout crowd, made it a great night for us.

Mehrts: **The French can fire up at any time. They're a pretty volatile team and we just assumed the worst going into the first test, that it would be one of those sort of games for them.**

Justin: It was a late night. The kickoff was at 8.45pm! That rocked me a bit. It makes for a helluva long day when you're waiting for a game of rugby.

Mehrts: The late kickoffs suit me, but I know Justin's not the only one who doesn't like them. Todd Blackadder certainly doesn't. But I quite like just cruising during the day leading up to the game, having a sleep if I feel like it.

You're supposed to stay up late, getting ready for a night game, so your body adjusts to the idea. That suits me too. I'm a night person. It's not often that I'd go to bed before 11pm, or 11.30. So I battle on tour when I'm with early sleepers.

I remember how I 'worked' Daryl Gibson pretty hard in Lille, because he's a guy who likes lights out at 10, or 10.30 at the very latest. He got pretty tired during the week. That old flat-footed shuffle got slower and slower as the week went on, as I slowly worked him.

Before the next test, in Marseilles, I was rooming with Byron Kelleher, and he was alright at night, although he's a terrible morning person.

There's something about halfbacks, they're awful morning people, like drowned rats. Rhys Duggan is terrible in the morning, Justin's not too good either. You never see Justin at breakfast, and Byron looks like he's fallen in the canal until it gets to about 11am.

Justin: We'd moved into a hotel on the outskirts of Paris, the Hotel de Warwick, for the game, and the trip into the ground probably should have taken well over an hour.

But in France you get the best police motorbike escorts in the world. I remember in 1995, when I first toured, the escorts were outstanding.

You don't want to get on the wrong side of them if you're a motorist. They were kicking the doors of people's cars, pushing them, pointing them to the side of the road, roaring at them with their sirens going.

They ride right up to a driver's window, bang on it, and give the driver a roar. So they cut our trip to the first test down to about 20 or 30 minutes!

If there was a revenge motive after the semifinal loss in the 1999 World Cup, it was on a personal level. It was certainly not a team oriented thing. The 1999 loss wasn't even discussed. But I'm sure there were a few people who were like me, wanting a bit of payback.

It was certainly a very different team playing in Paris from the World Cup semi, and in my case I hadn't actually played in the semifinal.

But I know that my main motivation for the first test was that I'd had to sit on the sideline and watch my World Cup dreams get destroyed the year before.

Now I had the chance to go out and play, and this time I wanted to give the French a taste of what it had felt like. Every test match you play is important, but a World Cup semifinal is even more important, especially when you know that you may only get the chance once to play in a World Cup.

Mehrts: For different guys the loss in the World Cup meant different things going into the Paris test.

As it happens, the World Cup game wasn't a real motivation for me. I've had a lot of disappointments and find that you can't make amends for them. For me, all I can do from a loss is to learn from the pain and try to make sure I never have that pain again.

Every time the All Blacks step out, you don't want to go through the pain again. So while the World Cup had been a loss, it was gone and the only connection for me was that I didn't want to see us lose to them twice in a row.

The media had been building it up as avenging the 1999 result and the last thing we wanted to do was to give any ammunition to the idea that nothing had changed in the All Blacks, and we hadn't moved on.

Justin: The Paris test, to tell the truth, wasn't a great game to play in. It was very stop-start, and Wayne Erickson seemed to blow up everything. As a player, it was a terribly frustrating game to be involved in, because every time you tried to get something going there would be a penalty or a scrum.

In Marseilles we'd all seen what sort of football the two teams were capable of if the game was left to flow, but he didn't let the game flow at all.

Most people felt that the game got better in the second half, and I'd agree that the ref wasn't quite as pedantic in the second spell, but really the whole game never got rolling.

Neither team got any pattern going. I know that from where I was, I felt that we were never able to get any momentum on, and that was largely due to the referee, although some of our mistakes didn't help either.

Mehrts: The French forwards were big and strong up front, so we couldn't expect to dominate them, but we certainly got stuck into our work and had a crack at it, which was really good.

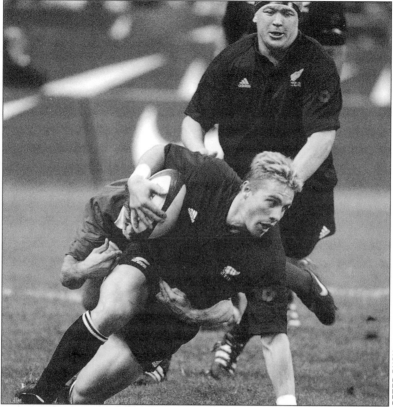

PETER BUSH

Justin's progress is stalled somewhat in action from the first test against France in Paris.

Early in the game I can remember looking at Christophe Lamaison when he was lining up his first couple of shots, and he has such a casual style. He just runs in, and 'bang', they're over.

In the World Cup he'd kicked a whole swag of dropped goals and penalties, and in Paris I was thinking, 'God, is this happening again? What is it with this guy? How does he manage that?'

He just wanders in with that typically French, almost blasé, slightly disdainful attitude. I guess they'd call it style. I find it amazing that some guys, like Lamaison, can concentrate

PETER BUSH

It's one for Dougie Howlett against the French in the first test at Paris and . . .

when they're still looking up at the posts while they're running in to kick.

Once I start running in I can't look away from the ball for a moment, but some guys start walking in and have a look up at the posts again. It's sort of spooky to me.

Justin: Still, at the end of the day we won the game, and Dougie Howlett's try was run in from a long way out and Christian Cullen's try was a good one, too.

There was some controversy over that one, with the suggestion there may have been a forward pass involved.

Mehrts: The pass from Jonah actually bounced off Olivier Magne's head, so there was certainly no forward pass. If you look at it closely on the replay that's quite clear, and it's the reason they didn't call Christian back.

PETER BUSH

. . . one for Christian Cullen in the same match. Tana Umaga's on hand to do the back-slapping.

Justin: I was reasonably annoyed about the last French try, to Fabien Pelous, at the time. I wasn't annoyed so much in the context of the effect it had on the game, because it wasn't going to affect the result.

But it was a prime example of a referee making a decision when he hadn't actually seen what happened, and on another occasion it could cost you a game. That was certainly the case in South Africa in 1998, when a try was awarded with the ball off the ground.

It's disappointing that's still happening. They really do need to have the video referee operating in all tests that are being televised. **For some reason, a third referee wasn't available for the tests in France.**

There might be some occasions when the third ref gets it

wrong, but at the end of the day he is going to get a better look at it, especially in slow motion, than a referee who makes a hasty decision on the ground.

You are certainly going to have more of a success rate with a video referee than with the man on the field guessing what happened.

Mehrts: The ball in Paris (for Pelous' try) was way high, miles off the ground, and I thought at the time that Wayne Erickson had blown for the try before the maul had even collapsed.

I get on well with Wayne Erickson. I like the guy as a person, and I think as a referee he knows what he's doing. But when there's a try like that you go, 'How the hell could he have seen that?' All we would ask as players is that a ref rules on what he sees.

As far as the whole game goes, I think that the ref probably wanted to keep it pretty tight, because perhaps he thought it could get a bit fiery, and he wanted to keep things right under control. **There had been a lot of talk after the World Cup last year that the French had used some dirty tactics. So perhaps he wanted to keep a very tight rein on things.**

In the end, I guess that if anyone benefited at all it would have been Lamaison and me – we got so many kicks at goal. During a game you don't keep a count of how many shots you've had, but even during the test I did know there had been a lot. I didn't realise how many there actually had been until after the test.

Justin: Although we won, it wasn't an exciting game to play in, and I'm afraid it wouldn't have been an exciting game to watch.

If there was excitement, the score being close would have had to provide it.

Mehrts: It was unfortunate that although we had the game under control for most of the time, conceding those two tries at the end left the guys feeling flatter than we should have been when we got back to the changing rooms. It just dulled it a wee bit. We knew that critics would fasten on later.

Looking back on it now, it was really a hell of an achievement to win in Paris on Armistice Day, but at the time we didn't get the satisfaction out of it that I think we will as time goes by.

Justin: The most notable difference with the aftermatch function in Paris from the way we do it in New Zealand was the fact that there was no beer at all. None. Just lots and lots of red wine, with cheese and crackers.

They do have the formal speeches with a translator for all of them. The guy had to find the French words for Toddy Blackadder thanking the ladies out the back for the great spread!

Mehrts: The boys were willing to make the ultimate sacrifice and have a crack at the wine. You know what they say, when in Rome. . . .

Justin: We then stayed on in Paris until the Wednesday when we flew out to Marseilles. We continued to train, but had a bit of free time when we got to the Lido.

Mehrts and I were lucky enough to go with Taine Randell and Andrew Martin to a restaurant called Guy Savoy, which has been voted one of the top five restaurants in the world.

Mehrts: Guy Savoy, himself, is a former rugby hooker, who has had a lot to do with French rugby. We'd been told that if you ever got an invitation to go to his restaurant you should leap at the chance.

There was no question that Taine had to go as the No.1 diner. When we go out, usually it's Taine who decides on how many courses, and what we'll have. Justin looks after the beers.

Justin: You don't get to one of those restaurants every day. In we walked for lunch, just as the wine was being popped open. We had 13 courses plus coffee, not to mention all the wine they threw down our throats.

Mehrts: There were some amazing things. I don't really like fish too much, but there was a whole fish in the middle of the table with herbs and vegetables in it, which was absolutely

PETER BUSH

In the lap of luxury. Former rugby player – and now leading restaurateur – Guy Savoy entertains us at his fine establishment.

superb. The pâté was amazing. It just went on and on.

Justin: It was French cuisine at its best, just an amazing experience, and I didn't go out of there 'chocker'. They bring out just enough for you to sample. They had some traditional French dishes, like rabbit they'd been cooking for six hours. That gets followed up by sorbets and so on, and we dined for three hours all up. We were very lucky, indeed.

Mehrts: It was an amazing experience. **I do remember thinking, 'This is a bit above me. I've got above my station here!' But it was one of those once-in-a-lifetime things you just had to experience. It was nice to see how the other half live.**

Justin: On the trip down to Marseilles, I was crook as a dog. I'd picked up a stomach bug from somewhere. We trained before we flew down, and I just lay on the back seat of the bus, with aching bones and feeling weak from throwing up.

The boys had gone out to train and I suddenly realised I was going to have to be sick. I went to get off the bus and found the driver had locked me in.

So I thought, 'There's a toilet on the bus'. I raced back to it and

found it, too, was locked. Now I was really desperate and I was flummoxing around, thinking, 'This is going to be messy', until I found somebody's kit bag. . . . That wasn't very pleasant and the trip down on the plane wasn't much fun for me, either.

Mehrts: I didn't know about that at the time. But some of the boys are so messy they wouldn't have noticed anyone had been crook in their bag.

Justin: We finally arrived and our hotel, the Hotel de Concorde Palm Beach, was built on the rocks at the edge of the harbour, which was a nice place to stay. Fortunately I recovered from the bug very quickly.

Mehrts: We had the day off on the Thursday, and I hopped on the train and went up to Grenoble to catch up with Mark and Jayne Mayerhofler. Mark's playing for the Grenoble club now.

Justin had recovered by the Friday and was able to play the test, although his digestive system was still playing a few tricks. I remember the day after the test he was striding to the bathroom doing a commentary on himself, saying, 'Marshall, about to reacquaint himself with the toilet for the first time since Wednesday'. Apparently all 'service' had shut down for a few days.

There was a bit of a shocker at the ground on the Friday. The French officials told us we weren't allowed to train on the ground as a team, but we were allowed to train outside and then walk over it as a team, and the goalkickers were allowed to kick.

The week before we'd gone well without much of a training run on the Friday, so we did the same again. We didn't have too much of a run at all.

So we went in to have a look at the ground, which is quite pleasant. The boys just float round, chuck a ball around and cruise through it.

We went to get a look at the changing rooms. It's a soccer ground, and there was a game scheduled for that night. That might help explain what went on.

The official in charge of the ground got very, very agitated and was convinced for some reason that we wanted to go into

PETER BUSH

Contretemps! Mehrts is the man in the middle of this altercation with the Marseilles soccer club. At right is Andrew Martin.

the Marseilles soccer team's home changing room. He wouldn't let us look at any of the changing rooms.

After two weeks in France I was starting to speak a wee bit of French. I did eight years of French at school and at varsity and, being in France for some time, I was able to understand a bit of what was going on.

At one point, the Marseilles official was saying, 'This is my house. You're trying to get into my house'. He was really asserting his authority.

The day before a game is usually my niggardly day, so I almost enjoy going to a ground and striking some silly guy who's being stupid and over the top.

I actually said to him, in my best French, 'What have you been taking this morning?' Because his voice had suddenly just gone hugely high and shaky.

Finally, they calmed him down enough to agree that we could go into the changing room we were going to use. But we were only allowed in six at a time. So when I got inside I was really giving it the old, 'Oh, now I see why you weren't able to let us in.'

We then went back outside and our French Rugby Federation liaison guy was there. He was a big, round guy, who looked like an actor playing a Capo in a Mafia movie.

He was sort of with us, but we didn't see a lot of him and he didn't speak any English. But he was a rugby man, and he was letting himself be worked over by the soccer guys at the ground.

Carlos Spencer had started to take a few shots at goal and our friend, the Marseilles official, came storming out and pushed one of the boys, I think Daryl Gibson.

So I started getting into an argument with the rugby guy who was with us. People in New Zealand saw a shot on the news of me calling him Marlon Brando. In French I accused him of being a puppet, dancing to the tune of the soccer officials.

The upshot of it all was that we ended up being shown off the ground. Some of the boys were a bit upset by it all, but for me it was actually a sort of release in some ways. It burns off a lot of nervous energy.

Saturday, November 18.

France beat the All Blacks 42–33 at the Stade Velodrome at Marseilles.

For the All Blacks: Tries by Justin Marshall, Doug Howlett and Gordon Slater; four penalty goals and three conversions by Andrew Mehrtens.

For France: Tries by Xavier Garbajosa, Olivier Magne and Fabien Galthie; five penalty goals, two dropped goals and three conversions by Christophe Lamaison.

Justin: There was another 8.45 kickoff. It was a hell of a game,

PETER BUSH

Taine Randell, Norm Maxwell and Mehrts prior to the start of the second test in Marseilles.

and in direct contrast to the test in Paris. The one in Paris didn't flow, but this boy flowed.

It flowed for them for the first 15 or 20 minutes, and then it flowed for us, and then it went backwards and forwards.

Mehrts: They just got away to a brilliant start. That Garbajosa is simply brilliant. Justin and I were pretty gutted about his try. He stutter-stepped down the blindside, stood up Justin, then chipped ahead past me, and with my comparative lack of gas I was out of it.

Then Olivier Magne just ran through one off a ruck. They had this huge backline and suddenly they hit this guy with a short pass and he was in. We were almost stunned, just looking at each other going, 'What the hell is happening here?'

Then we knuckled down, got hold of the ball, and got back into it. Maybe it's the five-point try, but you do often feel that at any stage you can get back into the game.

We just eked our way back into it and started using the ball a bit better – using space a little better. They've always been susceptible to turnovers, and to switches of play. We moved it wide, got it to Dougie Howlett, and he ended up cantering away.

Once we got on that sort of a roll we started to feel a bit more confident. I think the French had possibly eased up a bit, then they put the acid back on again and it was a bit of a ding dong for a fair while.

When you get back into the game, you try to keep playing the simple sort of rugby that had got you back; you're loath to change anything that's been working.

For most of the second half I still felt reasonably confident, especially when we hit the front in the second half. But then the French raised it again and we turned the ball over too much.

I was one of the culprits at one stage late in the game when we'd held the ball for five or six phases. I grubbered the ball through. They took it, whacked it downfield, and we were back on defence.

After the test the changing shed was very quiet. I can assure everyone that nobody hurts more than the players when we lose.

To be honest, the French are a very good side. It may be that the tests with us will be the peak of their season. They were at about the same stage of the season that we were when we beat the Australians in Sydney at the start of Tri-Nations 2000. You've had enough hard rugby to be in good shape, but you're fresh enough to have heaps of raw enthusiasm.

Justin: I was just gutted when the test was finished. I'd spoken before we left New Zealand about the inadequacies in our game, the way we'd been unable to finish teams off in the Tri-Nations when we had chances to win.

We'd talked as a team, and thought we'd got those things right, but unfortunately under pressure we still haven't got the experience and nous to put teams away when we get ahead.

We got ahead in Marseilles, but just let things slip. Everyone was deeply disappointed. We knew we had the game there to grab, take and win, but we let it slip. The French played well and we made a few mistakes because we were under pressure.

Although I was devastated that we didn't win, it was good to hear from home that people recognised it as a very exciting game to watch, even though we lost. Certainly playing the test, it felt like a very good game.

As a player, the disappointment if you lose is so great that often you don't recognise what a good game you've played in. On reflection, having seen the game, it was a cracker of a test and the French played bloody well.

We had our backs to the wall, down 17–0 early on, and I reckon the team showed some real character to keep coming back into it.

The day after the test I had to go to the media conference, which I really didn't want to, because I knew I'd be asked questions that I didn't really know the answers to.

Questions about the pressure. Questions over why we choke, what's going wrong? I didn't know. I knew I'd be asked that, and I also knew it would be ridiculous to sit there and say, 'We've got a really tough game coming up now with Italy'.

The fact is, we were expected to win against Italy, and you'd be naïve to think differently.

So it is tricky in that sense, but also what we did was look at it as a team.

It was decided that on the Monday, after a free day on the Sunday, we'd sit down and try to nut out what was going wrong.

Everybody in the squad believes in each other and we all believe in the team, so it's a matter of getting that last little bit just right.

We've all got to get that working. We thought we'd done that, but in Marseilles we found we hadn't. We had a good session, and from that session everybody got really motivated.

In the session we had as a team, the good thing that emerged was that everyone wanted to get out and make the test with Italy work.

Mehrts: The loss was a pretty gut wrenching result, and there was fallout from that, but we did have a responsibility to get ourselves back up and prepare ourselves as best we could for the next game.

Justin: The coaches said they'd pick the team later in the week, on the Thursday, and would pick the players who they thought were ready to play, based on how we performed at training.

That got the feeling of meandering into the last game of the season right out of the way, because everybody desperately wanted to be out there and playing after the session we'd had as a team.

Mehrts: I went onto the bench for the game with Italy and there was a feeling in the New Zealand media that I'd been axed. But Smithy has never lied to me and he assured me that wasn't the case.

Carlos had played well all season and he was coming back into the All Black environment after about 18 months away. Smithy felt he deserved to play.

I would have rather been playing, but I could understand where Smithy was coming from. He was straight up to me. He told me that it wasn't a reaction to the second French test, or a question of form.

But straight away I was being asked questions like, 'We know Wayne Smith says it's not a question of form, but surely you're being made to pay for an inability to follow a game plan'. So straight away that was how it was going to be reported.

Those sort of things become accepted fact, which I find a bit annoying. It can crop up later if you are dropped, and the reports would say, 'It's not the first time. Remember he was dropped for the game with Italy in 2000.'

Still, all I could do was get in and try to do my job, and do as much as I could to keep the team up as we prepared for Italy.

Saturday, November 25.

The All Blacks beat Italy 56-19 at the Stade Luigi Ferraris at Genoa.

For the All Blacks: Tries by Bruce Reihana (2), Ron Cribb (2), Doug Howlett, Filo Tiatia, Carlos Spencer and Justin Marshall; two penalty goals and five conversions by Carlos Spencer.

For Italy: Tries by Andrea Lo Cicero and Stefan Saviozzi; three penalty goals by Ramiro Pez.

Justin: I reckon the Italian forwards might have been tucking into a bit of that mad cow beef, because they sure came out swinging.

You don't usually see players lashing out like the Italians did after Filo Tiatia scored his try. We'd talked amongst ourselves about how we weren't going to be walked over by a team.

We decided that if people were going to ask the question of whether we were tough enough, we were going to have to stand up, and we'd have to stand up together.

When the fight started I was back on halfway, because I'd been on the ground. I'd got up and was walking back. **There was Troy Flavell and myself, and we were the only two people on the entire field who didn't get involved in the fight.**

I came running past him; he saw me go and he came bursting up to me again, but by the time we arrived the scrap was all over.

Mehrts: I was there fidgeting in the dugout when an unusual thing happened. About eight years before I had played in Italy for the Calvisano club, and whenever the All Blacks are in Italy, the boys from the club come across and catch up.

Once we were in Genoa I had a couple of mates, one a player from Calvisano, and the other a good friend from Christchurch who is now coaching there, come to see me.

We hung out together on the Friday before the test. We went

to a small café and had a coffee. Claudio, my Italian mate, hops on the phone and rings one of the Calvisano boys who's the two metre tall reserve lock for Italy, Luca Mastrodomenico.

So Luca comes down and we all have a coffee on the Friday afternoon. **Then, when the fight breaks out in the game, everyone stands up to have a look, and for a laugh I ran all the way down to the Italian bench.**

I'm standing in front of their bench, pointing at this giant lock, Luca, saying that I want a piece of him, that he was lucky I didn't get there a little earlier.

Initially I bet all the Italian officials wondered what the hell was going on, this skinny little Kiwi wanting to take on an Italian giant. We had a good laugh about it after the game.

Justin: The scrap is the sort of thing that many will say shouldn't be encouraged in sport, and that's right. But it's a bit like being in school, when there's a bully around. If you don't

Relative calm before the 'all-in'. Filo Tiatia is accosted by an irate Italian after his try, while Carlos Spencer locks on.

stand up for yourself, you'll get picked on. So we decided that if we were being picked on, we'd stand up for ourselves, and that was something that came out of the team meeting we had before we left France.

We had a lot thrown at us from the Italian team, and while there was a lot of negative, disruptive stuff, I was proud that we stood up and didn't let ourselves get bullied. It'll hopefully be a good lesson learned for us.

Mehrts: We know that it wasn't the ideal example to be setting, but for some time people have been suggesting we've got to be more hard-nosed. That doesn't mean being stupid and giving away penalties, but I don't think you can afford to take a backward step in those circumstances.

I was on for the grand total of two minutes at the end. I caught the ball once and threw a pass well in front of Doug Howlett, which went into touch. The Italians won the lineout and scored a try. So I wouldn't say it was my most auspicious moment in rugby.

Both: The initial plan for after the game was that we'd all have four days off, and then go to the adidas headquarters in Herzo, in Germany.

But not long before the tour it changed. **The Italian Rugby Federation wanted to host us in Rome and the New Zealand Ambassador invited us to a dinner.** So the four days free to do whatever you wanted to in Europe came down to two.

Mehrts: I was about the only one who didn't just go to Rome. I'd already organised that I'd go and see the Mayerhoflers again. It's a big move for them, especially with a two-year-old child. They've relocated everything, and are in a new country, with a foreign language.

I had two really good days there which went really quickly. I spent a lot of time with their son, McKenzie, watching heaps of videos.

Then we went back to Rome, where the New Zealand embassy dinner, at a rowing club, was actually very enjoyable. There weren't lots of speeches. We just hung out, talking with a few Kiwis who lived there and with some Italians who had an obvious Kiwi interest.

Justin: We were off pretty early on the Wednesday morning to Germany to meet with the adidas people.

We had a process where we all got split up and they went through the gear, the boots, the footballs and the sponsorship itself. We went over everything they wanted to do, and where they wanted to go, and what the players wanted from them.

It was a complete look at what adidas wanted from rugby, and what we wanted from them. We saw what went in to making our gear, and what they're doing to try to give us every advantage they can, even if it's half a per cent advantage.

They've got the technology there, and if we can get an edge from it, why not? It was a real eye opener to all of us.

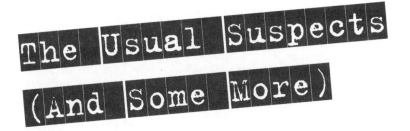

The Usual Suspects (And Some More)

There's no question that one of the great things about rugby is that you get the chance to go through a heap of things with your mates. Here's a rundown – in no particular order – of some of the people on the All Black scene as we see them.

JEFF WILSON'S personality lends itself to being in a position of authority, because on the field he's really intense. And guys who played with him in '93 say that he's actually loosened up a lot since then.

He's got a lot of desire, in an almost American sort of way. He's grown up playing a lot of basketball and he's got an in-your-face passion when he plays rugby.

Certainly he doesn't hold back at telling anyone what he thinks, which is a good thing. You don't want introverts in the team.

Justin: I've known Jeff for a long time, playing rugby and cricket in Southland against him, and then playing our first senior game for Southland together, against Canterbury. It was a pretty close game, but Shayne Philpott slotted a few goals against us.

'Goldie' was a fast bowler. I mean FAST. I was an opening fast bowler myself, and one of my best moments in cricket was

Jeff Wilson (at back), Mehrts, right, Anton Oliver and Tony Brown do battle on the card table.

playing in a regional team against Goldie. Everybody knew about him when he came in to bat.

I was off a long run, on a synthetic track. He had on pads, which straight away in Mataura is a bad sign, a helmet – with a visor – elbow guards, thigh guards on both sides, and a box. Everyone's going, **'Oh yeah, here comes Wilson'. I came charging in and the ball hit him in behind the pad and he had to go off.**

Mehrts: That story really amazes me . . . that I haven't heard it more often. You should listen to these guys talking about how good they were at cricket, how they want to get into the nets now and bounce each other to bits, send heads rolling all over the pitch.

Justin: Later on, of course, he was a New Zealand cricketer, but we really got to know each other when we started playing rugby together for Southland.

Mehrts: I've got a bit of an embarrassing confession to make about Goldie. When he first came through into the All Blacks I wondered if being a cricket star as well had helped his profile, and maybe helped get him into the All Blacks. I was actually a bit sceptical.

Once I played with him I really changed my mind. There are few better players than Jeff, anywhere in the world.

He can beat a man in more ways than most, but he can also draw and pass, and send a guy away.

Justin: He's really one of those players who, when you're playing against him, you have to watch all the time.

Both: Of course, it would be ridiculous not to mention that Goldie's a bit of a show-off after he scores a try. It's great that he's coming back.

CHRISTIAN CULLEN sleeps a lot. In fact, a lot of those really, really fast guys sleep a lot. Afato So'oalo in the Crusaders, Joeli Vidiri . . . they're all sleepers. They all sleep all week.

'Cully' is relentless. On the bus, in the room after training, anywhere, he's sleeping. It perhaps doesn't help that he looks like he's sleeping a lot of the time. That may be why some people get fooled into thinking he's not onto things, but he's sharp.

Cully's sometimes called 'Crowbar', because Taine Randell decided that you needed a crowbar to get the ball out from under his arm. He's quite happy with it now. He'll answer to that, or 'Bar', or 'C. Bar'.

We'll give him credit for having a finely tuned sense of humour, because down near the back of the bus he does laugh at most of the same things that we do.

JONAH LOMU, the big guy. He's a whopper. Big on everything. His money is big, his gadgets get bigger and bigger. His stories seem to get bigger as the years go by, too. How much he ate. Everything.

The first car he ever bought before he became really famous was a secondhand BMW, which was very nice . . .

before he turned it into a speaker on wheels.

He's got a cousin who has won Australasian loud car competitions, and with what Jonah's got now he's winning them here. **They reckon that if you sat in some of those cars and turned the volume up full, it'd stop your heart. So Jonah loves his cars, loves his music and combines them both.**

Jonah was the originator of the big headphones. A lot of the players turn up now for training with big headphones, but back in '95 he was the one who was allowed by Laurie Mains to arrive with them on. Broke down a lot of barriers.

He's the music committee, and he's pretty on to it. He chucks in a wide variety. Last year, for example, we were hearing Elton John and Kiki Dee, *Don't Go Breaking My Heart*.

We're all prepared to listen to a range of music. Tana and Alama were the kings of music in the hotels, and they lean towards dance and hip hop, while Greg Feek is more a heavy metal man. Goldie's into the '80s, like *More Than A Feeling*, but we'll always give another guy's music a spin.

We call Jonah 'Big Guy', but he calls himself 'Da Bomb'. The trouble is that because he decided that himself, nobody else calls him that. He's got Da Bomb painted on his car. One of the boys once asked who this D.A. Bomb guy was.

TANA UMAGA to us is 'Glenn McGrath', and he doesn't like that. So we keep calling him that. But that's about all we take the mickey out of him about, because he's one of those guys who just doesn't warrant it for some reason, which is disappointing.

He's a lot more quiet with the media and the public than he is inside the team, but basically he's just a good guy.

ALAMA IEREMIA had a bit of clout, being a back seat man until he headed to Japan. He's similar to Tana; he didn't get much targeting, just the odd occasion when you held up a stick of deodorant, and asked him if he'd lost his chapstick.

We called him 'Milan', and there's no explanation for where that came from. He was a real hard out guy on the field. You

PETER BUSH

Media-shy Tana Umaga offers a smile for ace lensman Peter Bush during the French tour.

just knew that you could rely on him and that he wouldn't ever let you down.

He was a real thorn in the side of the golfing committee, though. We usually play stablefords, where you put everyone's scores into a hat and draw out pairs. **He never lost at any golfing occasion. He played well himself, without his handicap coming down.** He used to win with Ravishing Richard Fry, who was our sponsorship manager. That was always annoying, because Richard actually organised the golf, and Richard never seemed to lose.

Justin: The other really distinguishing feature with Alama was his phone. Four of us went out with him when we were in Tauranga, and I'd never seen it before. He had one of those cords that you just ran up the side of your neck. **So we're just walking down the street, and he's there with his sunnies on, just talking away, sort of into his shirt collar.** I'm looking around to see who he's talking to. I thought he must have been singing to himself. Then we went into a restaurant, ordered hamburgers, and sat down.

He started doing it again. He's got his head down, talking away flat out in Samoan. He looked like he was in a movie like *In The Line of Fire.* He's massive on the phone, and he's on it all the time.

Mehrts: I consulted him all the time over Samoan. Afato So'oalo has taught me some Samoan, but I think it might just be the rude stuff. You want to make sure with some of those big Samoan guys that you're not causing offence.

Don't ever expect Alama to be a guest on breakfast television with Mike Hosking. We were all at a Warriors game in Auckland once, and one of the boys jerked Alama over Mike Hosking's name. So, for the whole afternoon Alama's calling Mike Hosking 'Dave'. 'How are you, Dave? – Good game Dave'.

DARYL GIBSON is a prolific Coke drinker. He made the statement that Big Guy was a bigger Coke drinker than him, but we question that.

When he wakes up in the morning he has a can of Coke. He would get through four or five a day just sitting in his room, plus whatever he has when he has lunch.

'Gibbo' is a good thinker on the game, knows his patterns, and he's sharp. He's a really balanced runner, with plenty of skill. Being so versatile, he's always had to play in a variety of positions until he was on tour with the Maori team at the end of '98 when Mark Mayerhofler was injured, and Gibbo got the chance to settle in at second-five, where he went really well, and then grabbed another chance in Super 12 in '99.

He's been a really important part of the Canterbury side for ages, because although he's been moved around, he's so good he can't be just left on the bench. He's such a good thinker on the game, he can read the game in whatever position he's placed.

Mehrts: Gibbo was two years behind me at Boys' High. I think the only reason he didn't play in the First XV with me in my year there was that they thought he was too young as a fifth former.

He's got an uncanny knack of agreeing with everything I say, even when we don't know what the other may have just said. It might be video refs, let's say. Justin's all for them, and I'll come storming into a room at the tail end of the discussion and say, 'That's just rubbish', and Gibbo will go, 'I just said that'. Unbelievable the number of things that have cropped up that we agree on. The guy's right as often as I'm right, and Justin's wrong!

Justin: I set about breaking Gibbo down when we were in Pretoria. I was rooming with him for five days. I made a pledge at the first dinner when I told the team, 'I'm going to find out what makes Daryl Gibson tick.' How did I set about it? By asking subtle questions, like, 'Hey Gibbo, what makes you tick?'

I can reveal that, as well as Coke, he takes a terrible lot of Berocca, and forgets to flush the toilet, which means you're often likely to be dazzled by the orange glow. It can be the darkest day, but there are still rays of sunshine coming out of the toilet.

Mehrts: Kees Meuws does the same thing, but he passes it off by saying that he goes to the toilet a lot during the night, and he doesn't want to wake anybody up.

Justin: To be fair, with the length of the nose he's got, Gibbo probably never smells anything in the bathroom. It's almost certainly too close to him. On the other hand he can probably wake up in the morning, on the fourth floor of the hotel, take a sniff, and tell you whether it's bacon and eggs or sausages for breakfast.

Both: We call him 'Leonard', or 'Lenny', for Leonard Maltin, the movie critic. Daryl Gibson is an avid movie watcher, and he has very strict criteria on reviewing movies. He doesn't hedge his bets. It's never, 'Yeah, it wasn't too bad'. He's very tough if he doesn't like a movie. It's like, 'Poor actor, very weak storyline, didn't like it.'

TAINE RANDELL is the sort of guy who can't be serious all the time. **He's a funny guy who's at his best when he's totally himself.** It sounds so much better when he just says what he feels, like the way he took the mickey out of himself a bit after he'd put through the chip kick that led to the try for Cully in Christchurch in '99.

In '98 people suggested that the senior players weren't giving him the support he deserved as a captain, but that's not really true. At the end of it, the only support any of us could give him was to win the games. So he would have probably questioned everything he did, which was just not fair on the guy.

But there was never any division in the team. **There was never any questioning of his authority. There was never any arguing on the field, from the older guys, or anyone.** Any stories that suggested there were problems on those lines were crap.

Mehrts: What does happen when things are going wrong is that everything potentially seems a problem. The South Africans found that in '99. If they'd been winning everything then all the nonsense about Mallett talking about Montgomery's hair, or divisions between the provinces, would never have gone on.

Justin: Taine reckons he's one of the three funniest guys in the team.

Mehrts: We disagree. We reckon he's a bit one-dimensional. We're first equal, and Norm Maxwell's third.

Justin: At best, Taine's fourth.

Mehrts: He's a bit too clever, and he struggles to drop himself to a lower level of humour at times.

Justin: Mind you, he is fast.

Mehrts: And he is the best at computer games. Very quick.

MARSHALL & MEHRTENS

Justin is alert, but is no doubt aware he's about to get another computer game bashing at the hands of Taine Randell.

Justin: That's true. You know the games where two guys play against another two guys? In the Otago team Jeff Wilson and John Blaikie teamed up, and the two of them were attacking Taine. He beat both of them. That's really irritating.

Mehrts: He's so organised on the computers, which is in stark contrast to his room, which is so messy.

Justin: He stayed at my place in Christchurch, and he came with one small bag of gear. Overnight, with just that one bag, he turned the room into a flippin' bomb site. **There were undies out in the hallway, socks on the wardrobe. I think he must come into a room, open his suitcase, lift it up, and keep shaking the clothes out until the room's covered.**

It's odd that he's so disorganised in that regard, because the three of us, Taine, Mehrts and Justin, were the laundry committee in France and Italy in 1995. We got big hats made, saying 'Laundry Boss', and while the current group do a pretty good job, we claim that we set the benchmark in '96.

Taine was an integral part of that committee, and it'd be unfair not to say that players in '96 ran no chance of letting themselves or their team down by being hit by a bus and having to go to hospital in grubby undies.

We have to say that he's got some real backbone in the clothing area, too. Nomads went out 10 years ago, but he's still wearing them. Same thing with bomber jackets.

Naturally, Taine will never be allowed to forget the famous *Sunday News* photo of him and a couple of the guys about to go for a swim. Some say that it wasn't a flattering photo of Taine because he looked a bit tubby in it, but it's our belief the photo actually flattered him.

Taine took it pretty well, although it's tough to believe his claims that the rippling washboard stomach he now has is the result of two years of discipline and hard work on his sit-ups and other exercises.

He says he bought one of those ab machines they advertise on TV, but that it didn't really work, so he put it in the closet. Mind you, it wouldn't have been getting much work sitting in the closet.

Naturally, after the *Sunday News* photo, he's been answering to the name 'Teapot', as in, 'I'm a little teapot, short and stout. . . .'

When we did the Army camp last year we were in two groups, with one having a tug-of-war and the other climbing up ropes. You had to use different methods to climb up the ropes and slide down.

Now Taine is the worst man for chin-ups. He's told us that in the fourth form he could do two chin-ups. In the fifth form he could do two. In the sixth form he could do three. In the seventh form he could do three. Now we get tested for them in the All Blacks, and he did four.

So he's at the Army camp, with these Army guys yelling at us all, and Taine gets to the ropes, and he's giving it a real nudge, really digging it in, and he can only get halfway up the rope. So he slides down and runs across to the tug-of-war.

Now he's smoking. He's the anchor man and he wraps the big rope round him. Great at that. Then he has to go back to climbing between the two ropes. Straining, straining. Back down and over to the tug-of-war. The Army guys are screaming, but he's the master of the tug-of-war, not climbing ropes and chin-ups.

But hey, it doesn't matter. As long as he does the job on the field – and he does – then who cares?

JOSH KRONFELD, alias 'Crusher'. Actually Crusher was a name that Josh didn't like. It may have just been a name that came from a commentary once. It became 'Russia', became 'Crunch', became 'Lunch', became 'Flush', anything really. Nicknames are just open season. There are no undercurrents though, no hidden agendas.

Mehrts: I've had to come to grips with 'Don't Cut Your Hair'. **I'd be the first to say that I'd never pretend to have a fashionable haircut, but in '97 it was really long and horrible, and we were watching a midweek game, when some English guys down in front noticed us and started chanting, 'Andy, Andy, Don't Cut Your Hair', so it's become 'Don't Cut', or whatever.** It's not worth fighting it. If you show you don't like it, then you're doomed. The team will always be stronger.

Both: Josh is a real individual, and loves to be seen as such. He would, along with Anton Oliver, be the rugby guy most in denial from the All Blacks. Just in denial about being a rugby head. He will refuse to watch it, and would hate to be seen as a conformist.

With Josh, you can bring up any subject you like and he will have a story or some sort of related topic about it. He knows a lot about a lot of things. You mention something in passing and Josh will be able to talk about it, and actually know what it is he's discussing.

He's always loved what he does away from the game, like surfing, playing the harmonica, and he's good at them, so he has the chance to get away from everything.

Justin: I remember going to watch him at the Outback Pub in

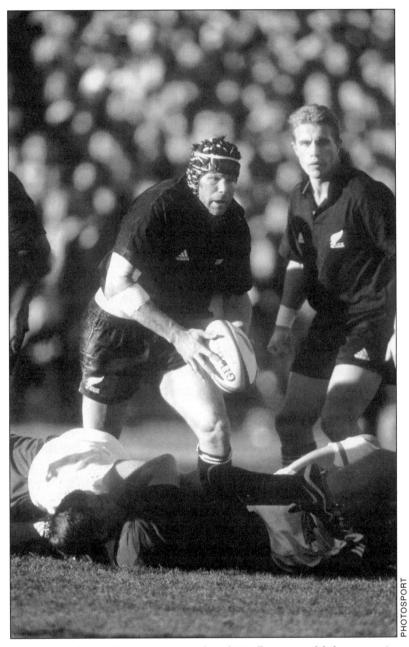

PHOTOSPORT

Josh Kronfeld – long arms and pointy fingers which seem to help him snaffle the ball.

London with Midge Marsden. I knew he could play the harmonica, but to get up in front of a pretty big crowd was impressive. I'd had a few diesels, but it still sounded good.

Both: On the field he always took the most punishment of anyone in the team. The ball he got through turnovers was great for us, because what he got was unexpected.

We got to see him at close hand, so we probably appreciate him even more than people in the crowd watching the game. He's amazing. **When you played against him he was the guy that you'd tell your team, 'Just forget anyone else, just blow him out of the way'. He's got long arms and pointy fingers, which seem to help him snaffle the ball.**

Mehrts: I would have to say that Josh only ever got annoyed on the field when he believed he was being penalised wrongly. When he played against Canterbury I think he was wrong a lot of the time. In fact, I'd suggest that I'm the tackled ball expert.

Justin: That applies to specialist on the rules in general. You certainly appear to know them better than every referee we strike.

Mehrts: That's true. It is a frustrating game for me! Seeing a man with less knowledge than I have calling the game.

Both: Josh's a pretty placid individual. **When we try to get into him he just shrugs it off and wanders away. Which is annoying.**

He's a slightly messy sort of guy, which is surprising. For some reason you'd think he'd be organised, but things tend to stay where they were dropped.

Mehrts: The first time I roomed with him I went into the bathroom to get my toothbrush, only to find a pair of his white Y-fronts draped over my toilet bag. He must have just whipped the undies off to get into the shower, biffed them, and they hooked over my toilet bag. Which is NOT ideal.

DYLAN MIKA took over the laundry duties in the team in 1999, and did a good job. In fact, we reckon it was the best laundry service since '95, when Randell, Marshall and Mehrtens were the laundry committee.

Dylan's a good pool player, and would have spent a lot more

time on the table if Mark Hammett and Carl Hoeft weren't there, playing one of their never-ending series of games. They play a series of five games, and they just count the series. Before we left for the World Cup last year they were up to about 44–42 in the series.

Dylan's a big man, with big hits on the field, and he's got an extremely deep voice. There's not a lot of oil on Dylan, but he is a whopping eater. Two of the biggest eaters in the All Blacks in recent times have been Dylan and Royce Willis.

Justin: I once went out for a meal with a group that included Dylan and Royce. Dylan ordered a massive burger, a toasted sandwich, a couple of pieces of fish and chips, then started to eye up Royce's meal opposite.

Royce had done exactly the same, and these were whopping feeds I'm talking about. Then Royce asked if I was going to finish my fish, and cleaned that up. Then Dylan finished and was looking around for more. It was like a boxing match, swapping mouthful for mouthful.

Mehrts: There's always been a lot of pride in the team over who can eat the most. Big Guy (Jonah) claims the biggest records, but as yet they're unverified.

Justin: I'd suggest some of those stories are untrue. Fifteen Big Macs?

Mehrts: And Jonah says, 'That's only for starters. Then I pick up a 20 piece bucket of KFC on the way home'. **The most we've ever ACTUALLY seen is Anton Oliver eating eight Big Macs, which is about 24 bites total.**

ANDREW BLOWERS, or 'AB', could often be found in his room using his Swiss ball, doing exercises or sit-ups, or making protein shakes, or being nice to someone. We reckon that in the bus on the way to the ground he'd hop out and help an old lady across the road.

Justin: I was sitting in my room once, and went to make a cup of tea. I said, 'Aw, there's no milk in the fridge'. AB says, 'Do you want some milk, bro? I'll get some'. I thought he had some in his room. He went all the way down to reception.

Both: AB was on the information committee, but the group was poor – the worst ever! The info committee was first brought in during '96 in South Africa. Glen Osborne was a one-man committee, and he was a classic. He'd read up the papers, read all the business tips, and then he'd deliver his report on the bus.

Oz used it mostly, though, to have on Frank Bunce and Walter Little. He'd say, 'And Ozzy's business tip of the day: Don't lend any money to Frank or Walter.'

But then they appointed AB and Norm Maxwell. AB was the researcher and Norm was going to present it to the team. But mainly Norm just told a few jokes, and that became a standard routine in itself. As soon as the information committee started, everyone else in the bus hopped up and hurled abuse.

To be fair to AB, he'd probably been busy helping everybody else on every other committee.

ROBIN BROOKE was to us, anyway, 'Bully'. That's because he made the mistake of telling us one day that, when he was a kid at school in Warkworth, he was a bit of a bully.

Mehrts: In fact, he's an awesome guy. A lot of people in Canterbury love to hate him, and I've had people over the years who ask me whether they think he hit me deliberately when I took a bad fall in a '94 Ranfurly Shield game against Auckland.

But once you get to know him you see what a superb guy he is, with a real ability to laugh at himself. It ends up that some of the guys from Auckland are the best you could meet.

I grew up in a culture in Canterbury where a lot of the Auckland players, like Mark Carter, were the real bad boys. But Mark Carter is one of the best roosters you could ever meet.

Both: Robin's much like Zinny in terms of competition. Most of the guys in the team are very competitive. Get a group of All Blacks standing around, and there'll soon be a game, like throwing darts into the floor, rolling coins

Striking a pose in one of numerous McDonald's outlets the All Blacks have frequented over the years is Rob 'Bully' Brooke.

around . . . whatever. Just so you can compete.

We were on a shuttle bus at an airport once, getting ready to go out to training, and Greg Feek and Mark Hammett were bouncing a ball, trying to get it to bounce on two pipes and then bouncing it straight up.

Rob starts watching them, and you could see his eyes going, trying to work out exactly what they were doing. Then he starts to ease across, inching closer, and in the end he tussles Mark Hammett out and starts playing. He won't stop until he gets it.

Zinny and Rob are slightly different personalities. Zinny's probably more assertive, but Rob, in his own way, is just as strong. Rob was a very well respected guy inside the team. He's always thinking about the game, and he often comes up with ideas on how to do things slightly better.

NORM MAXWELL took a few weeks to feel relaxed in the All Blacks, because he's very shy. It was much the same when he first came to Christchurch.

PETER BUSH

Stormin' Norm Maxwell, aka 'Maxi Taxi', brushes aside Stormers winger Breyton Paulse during the Super 12.

He's an amazingly gifted footballer, and once he felt okay he had some great things to offer. **People who meet him for the first time might feel that he was quite inarticulate, but that's far from the case.** He's very switched on, and really sharp about what's going on.

On the field he has enormous tenacity. There aren't many locks who get chucked up so high in the lineout, and make such an effort to get the ball, if it's not thrown to where they want it to be. He just makes an absolute effort to get everything, and he's got such incredible ball skills he often gets it.

This guy is 100 per cent for the team when he's out there. He starts off like a maniac, and he sustains it through the whole game. If you watch him closely, you'll see how much he does. You have to be astounded by the amount of work he gets through, and the number of tackles he makes.

Norm can show some of us what you can be capable of.

Norm's not a great big solid guy by any standard, but he knocks anybody around.

Once people feel good in the team, there are no divisions off the field between the guys who have had a lot of academic schooling and anyone else. **You start to see that in many cases that's just a load of crap. It's the EQ, the emotional quotient, that counts, how people deal with other people and read situations.**

Norm doesn't worry about what outsiders feel about him. With the Crusaders he'd often forget one or both of his black dress shoes. So he'd take the studs off his rugby boots and wear them to the aftermatch because they're black. No socks, just the black boots.

Normie is the messiest guy in the All Blacks. Taine's bad, but Norm's even a cut above that.

Norm is also the only man to our knowledge who, in one of John Hart's pre-match talks, has actually broken wind. We were in our Auckland hotel before a night test against Australia, and Harty had gone through the highs and lows, reached some crescendoes, and was nearing the end.

Normie must have taken in the bits that were relevant to him, and was into his own wee world in a way, as you sometimes are before game. Then he gave it the old, 'Baaarrp!'

Just as well we had our heads in our hands because every player in the room heard it, and our shoulders were just shaking with laughter. To his credit, Harty just carried on. Or perhaps he didn't hear it.

Norm has a penchant for giving himself names. One day it was 'Big Boy', and then he decided he wanted to be 'Taxi', as in 'Maxi Taxi'.

ROYCE WILLIS has a haircut that apparently came from the character 'Iceman' in the movie *Top Gun*, but as a guy you can't really fault him. He's goes really hard every time he's on the field, and is one of those genuine people who becomes mates with everyone in the team.

He's known as 'The Whopper', and he's not just big, he's

strong. When we went to the Army camp at the start of 1999 we had to carry ammunition boxes, and they were really heavy. **Justin:** Rhys Duggan and I were in Royce's group, and Rhys and I really struggled to lift the ammo container up. **Then Royce walks up, picks it up, puts it on his shoulder, and walks away.** Of course, while he was great at the things that needed strength, it was a real problem when he had to walk across things that might break. He was weighing in at about 125kg at that stage.

Mehrts: He's a scary man when he runs on the field as a sub. He came on at Eden Park once, sprinting, and there was almost a whoosh when he came flying past. Robin Brooke reckoned even he was a bit jittery after Royce had raced past him.

IAN JONES, or 'Kamo', was the last man to sit in what became called the ejection seat on the team bus. In buses now there's not really a back seat; they have a couple on each side of the toilet. **Robin Brooke was sitting in the outside seat on the right and Kamo in the far left seat. Then Kamo missed a cut, and went into the New Zealand A team. From that day nobody in the team would sit in the seat.**

Kamo's had a wealth of experience, and from that he had a lot to offer to the team.

CARL HOEFT, the old 'Bulldog', has a great set of teeth. The Otago boys reckon that he gets nervous when he goes to South Africa in case the ivory hunters get to him.

Mehrts: I was in a small group with him at the SAS camp and he's just an awesome guy, the first in the line when there's any work to be done. You can't fault him.

Both: He's someone you have a lot of respect for because when it comes to his job in the team he goes about it so well, and so professionally. He's immensely strong. If the scrum isn't working, there are problems right through the team, and he prides himself on making sure the front row is operating the way it should be.

If there is something not working the way it should, he

doesn't blame one single person, just works through what's happening until the problem's sorted out.

He does crack himself up every now and then with his own wee jokes. We were on part of a Neil Finn video in '99. Somebody needed a top for a part of the video so everyone would look the same, and Doc Mayhew took his top off and came across stripped to the waist to loan it. Hoefty goes, 'It's not THAT sort of video Doc . . . ha, ha, ha, ha'. He just cracked up at his own joke, and then everyone was falling about because he found it so funny.

His favourite joke is, 'Who is the lightest All Black of all time? Arf-a Stone! Ha, ha, ha, ha, ha, ha'. That's his trademark.

KEES MEUWS, or, as he calls himself, 'Bad News Meuws'. Or, as we call him, 'Sunday Meuws'. Or 'One Network Meuws'. Or 'Did You Hear The Meuws?'. Or 'Radio Network Meuws'.

He approaches the game a lot like Hoefty when it comes to the basics, although he does love running with the ball – at training, and in a game. He's very strong and explosive, an extremely good player.

Compared to Hoefty, there's a more in your face aspect to Kees. He's an individual who likes doing different things, and is something of an artist away from the game. He's probably more of an individual than the rest of us rugby heads.

ANTON OLIVER is 'Hatchet', or, to Mehrts, 'Two Bottles'. **That started when he was asked once whether he'd be buying Mehrts a drink, and he said, 'Yeah, but it'll be a cheap night. Two drinks and he's under the table'.**

Mehrts: He's a beast physically. I remember rooming with him in Taupo at the start of '98 and he took his shirt off. He was wandering round the room like Lou Ferrigo, the Incredible Hulk. Then I took my shirt off and it was Mr Bean meets the Hulk.

Both: Of all the guys, Hatchet is probably the one who most dislikes being thought of as a rugby head. He calls rugby

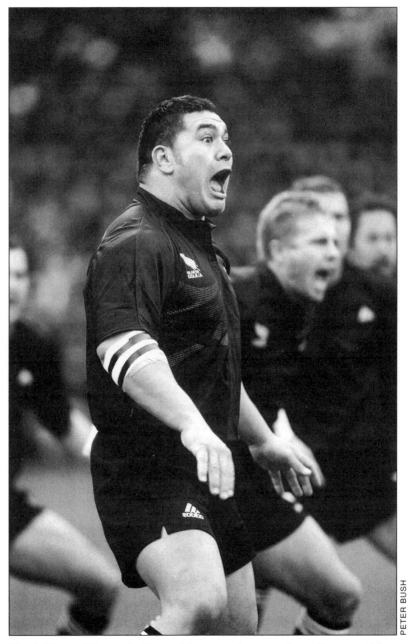

PETER BUSH

'Bad News Meuws'. Kees Meuws always gives it everything during the haka.

'code', and claims that he doesn't watch it on TV. If he walks into a room and we're watching a game he says, 'Aw, you're not watching code again, are you?' We reckon he's in code denial. So he's easy to get a bite from, you just claim that he's a rugby head.

Actually, he is pretty well rounded, which must go back to his days as a student in Dunedin. And he's well advanced for his age in the team and for the responsibilities he takes on. **He was only 19 when he was called into an All Black team in Australia as a reserve at the Sydney Football Stadium, so although he's still young now for a front rower, everybody in the country sees him as a leader in the All Blacks, and expects him to shoulder big responsibilities, which he does.**

There are players around him who may be a bit older than him, but he's charged with making sure the scrum works well. He works hard and trains hard and has a no-nonsense approach to footie.

When you just see him, he looks like a pretty tough sort of rugby forward, but he's a really nice, friendly, easy-going guy who yarns really easily with people. On the field he's probably one of the fairest players. He might get 'blown' occasionally for holding onto the ball too long on the ground, but basically he doesn't cheat.

MARK HAMMETT: 'Hammer' is thrilled to be there as the third Marsh twin. The Marsh boys, from Counties, Glen and Tony, and Hammer all look an awful lot alike, so we give Hammer a certain amount of stick about that. Hammer takes it all the chin, which is no problem, as there's a fair bit to spare.

Hammer's a bit like Anton – really hard on the field, and a really genuine, easy to get along with kind of guy off it. He's got a massive, natural booming laugh that you can hear anywhere in a room.

He got chucked in early to the Canterbury team, coming on to face the Auckland front row in '92 when he'd only just turned 20, and he's thrived on a challenge ever since.

Mehrts: I met a guy called Mark on Mona Island in Fiji, a huge, strong guy who used to play a lot of sevens rugby. He said, 'When you are back to Christchurch, I assume you know the Hammett brothers, Mark and Chris'. I said that I did, and he said to give his best to them, especially Mark. Apparently the team from the island, who were famous for sevens, played in a tournament in Christchurch, and had thrashed everyone until they faced Marist.

Apparently, the Hammetts decided that the bigger they were, the harder the Hammetts would smash into them with their tackling. They just flew into them. Mark, the Fijian, said he still had the bruises in his ribs four years later.

Both: That's how Hammer likes it, the harder the better, which is why he loves playing against South African teams. When he scored against Natal in Super 12 in '98, that was very Hammer, fending off a couple, and having a real go.

GLEN OSBORNE was best known in the All Blacks for his comments from the back, abusing the music committee. As soon as they put on a song, you'd hear this voice going, 'We've already heard that song. This is a STINK tape'.

'Oz' certainly lifted the music profile for the All Blacks when he returned for the World Cup in '99, because we were seriously lacking in guitar-playing ability, which he certainly brought to the side.

Most people would already have worked out Oz's personality from what they've seen on TV. **He's a true country boy, with eels in his back yard. There's a stream he catches them from, and he loves them smoked. He into all that kind of stuff – eels, lambs' tails, kina. Beautiful.**

Oz was a great guy to have in the team. You'd never hesitate to try and find him, because he's just great company and always positive. If you saw him a couple of blocks down the street, you'd yell out and run to catch up with him. You can't help but smile the second you hear his voice.

There have been some classic Oz moments. He was on *Friday Night Footie* on television, and was asked how many people he had staying at his home. You could see what he was

Glen Osborne on video patrol during the '99 World Cup. 'Oz' shaped as one of the great characters of All Black rugby.

thinking, that there were three people as well as himself. But Oz goes, 'There's three. Me, my wife, and our two children!'

He's spent a lot of time in that culture of the sevens teams, with Eric Rush and those guys, so he's always thinking of ways to jerk you. But there's never any malice.

Frank Bunce told us about a billboard the North Harbour boys were being photographed for. The billboards had Auckland on one side, and the Harbour players on the other, with all of them dressed in cowboy gear.

Buncey and Oz and the Harbour boys were fooling around with their hats, and Oz turned his sideways. He asked how it looked. The Harbour guys all kept a straight face and said, 'Awesome, keep it like that'. So when the billboard finally appeared with Oz on it, his hat was sideways, and his two big eyes were peering out from under it. Nobody knew if it was an ad for rugby or *The Muppets*!

On top of it all, Oz is a great player. If you knew that Oz was

PETER BUSH

Sheer bliss. Pita Alatini puts on the 'moves' for the All Blacks against Scotland this year.

playing or coming on, you had complete confidence in him. People tended to forget how quick he was, because he had such a long stride. He could really gas it. **You look at the try he scored for New Zealand A against the Australians last year. He gassed it, then stepped, then gassed it again for the try. He's a brilliant finisher, with a great step.**

PITA ALATINI, or 'Ala', or 'Mr Bliss', is a great team guy – always enthusiastic, always smiling, always trains well. He's one of those guys who you find it hard to dig any dirt on.

Justin: He does take a fair bit of pride in his appearance. I once roomed with him in Auckland and he spent a fair bit of time with his family. But I have to say his bed was always covered with 'product' – shampoo, conditioner, hair gel, the works.

He's a bit of a mover. I guess with his partner, Megan, being in True Bliss he has to keep up with what's going on in the music world. When something he likes comes on the

PETER BUSH

Highlanders and Otago team-mates Tony Brown and Taine Randell. 'Brownie' is a natural sportsman.

radio I always noticed that Ala was grooving along to it. I have been out and seen Ala and Megan dancing, and obviously she can really dance, so I guess he has to make sure he's not left behind.

Mehrts: It's not quite like the Mataura two-step shuffle!

TONY BROWN is a classic. **A straight out amusing guy, who is good at everything.** He's obviously good at rugby, good at cricket – it doesn't matter. Basketball hoops, golf, the lot. You could go crazy trying to find something he can't master. Go out for golf with him and he just walks up, no preamble, whacks it and away it flies.

Mehrts: He hits the ball incredibly hard and long at golf. We were playing together one day and I said, 'We'd better find your tee'. 'Brownie' said, 'I don't care what's happened, just as long as it disintegrated.'

Both: He's a good guy who fits in really well. But there is just one true, Just-Like-Mehrts, spit the dummy, absolute first-five behaviour story.

Justin: This is what happened. We take a cricket bat on tour, and play in hallways, wherever we can. We were playing in a conference room, with Taine, Gibbo, Anton, Tony and myself. Tony was batting.

He went forward to a shot, pushed at it, and it went behind. Taine was the wicketkeeper, and he gave it the big shout, 'Howzzzatt?' A second later the rest of us go up too, and we all start clapping. There was no sound, but we all say, 'You're out Brownie'. But he refuses to go out.

He says, 'I didn't touch it. Honesty call'. We're all, 'No, bad luck, we all heard it, you're out, caught behind'. But he won't go. 'Come on, guys, at least let me throw the bat up, and rule it that way'. We all say, 'No, that's it. You're out. There's no two ways about it. You're gone.'

It goes on and on, and finally he throws the bat down, kicks the wickets over and says, 'You can stick your bloody cricket', and away he goes.

Everybody's name is on a blackboard with their runs on it, and we proceeded to rub his name out. Then, in South Africa later in the year he came back asking if he could play again, and Taine said, 'No, you can't play because you're a dummy spitter.'

Mehrts: I didn't realise this had gone on, and I was at training and these guys were calling him 'Dummy' and I had no idea why until later. He was fired up. But on behalf of all first-fives I'd just like to say I can understand why.

CARLOS SPENCER is a guy who is very misunderstood by people in the south especially. **There's an assumption that 'Los' is arrogant and might strut around. But that's absolutely untrue. He's actually a really quiet guy.**

The only time we don't like him is when he's on the reserves bench for a game. At training, when the reserves are running at us, Los switches play, does all his tricks, and makes us look

PHOTOSPORT

Carlos Spencer is a multi-talented rugby player – here he shows off his place-kicking skills for the All Blacks.

ridiculous on defence. He might wait for a while, then flick it to Jonah and then 'boomp' – he'd knock a couple over.

Mehrts: There's also an assumption that Los and I don't get on, but we get on fine. He tended to hang out with guys like Oz, while I might be playing cards with Justin, but we were never unfriendly towards each other.

Los is a pretty fun sort of guy, but not in an 'out there, in your face' sort of way. He'll be sitting in the background with a bit of a grin on his face.

He's an awesome player, and so dangerous. No matter how the media might bag him, Los is a bit like Jonah. They don't worry about what's being written about them; when you're playing against them you can't relax for a moment.

Jonah will take three or four guys to look after him, and Los needs almost as many. He's got so many skills and so many ways of beating a man.

Justin: He's a hard trainer, too. Does lots of sit-ups and things like that. He's another guy who makes lots of healthy milkshakes and eats lots of protein bars.

There's not much oil on him. He's keen on his golf, and he's very good at it. But, in general, he keeps his nose pretty clean.

BYRON KELLEHER is 'Wozzer' to the team. Let's explain the nickname. When Crusher came back to Otago from a trip away with the All Blacks, Byron had come into the Otago squad. **Crush asked one of the guys what the new halfback's name was. The other guy had his mouthguard in. He said, through the mouthguard, 'Ith's Bywon'.**

Josh thought he'd said, 'Warren'. So he called him Warren for about a month. Nobody told Josh, and Byron, being new, didn't like to step up and say, 'My name's bloody Byron'. So Warren became Wozzer.

The standard thing with Wozzer when he first came into the team was that he was always on the phone, talking to his partner, Andrea. He got teased a bit about that, and we tried to name him 'Telecom', but he shrugged that off.

Justin: The main thing about Byron is that he's an honest, all heart guy. He played his way into the All Blacks with a great Super 12 in 1999, and every chance he's had with the All Blacks he's seized.

The Otago boys give Byron heaps because they know him better, but in general he gets on well with everyone in the squad.

REUBEN THORNE is the original strong, silent type. But when he gets a few 'steams' in him he wants to wrestle with everyone.

When he does say something, it's worth waiting for. He's a bit like Hoefty. When there's work to be done, he's the first in line.

Mehrts: Reuben goes out with my sister, and when I see him at home, at a family get together, it's quite funny. **The Mehrtenses just overrun him in conversation. Everyone is just chipping, chipping, chipping, and Rueben goes, 'Yeah'.**

Justin: Then there's a big silence while the male Mehrtens get the hiccup thing over with.

Mehrts: My old man and I both do that when we're talking. We're going flat out, then we stop, hold the stomach, big swallow and carry on. It's become quite a feature of after-dinner conversation.

Both: He can surprise you sometimes. **For some reason he doesn't seem to be a guy who'd be a Playstation man, but he enjoys his** *Shane Warne Cricket*, **just sitting and playing it quietly, of course.**

Mehrts: I've played a lot of football with Reuben at the Old Boys club in Christchurch, and he's always been the same. Hard yards, awesome on defence, and a very underrated attacker.

SCOTT ROBERTSON: 'Razor' is Mr Positive, almost larger than life. If he's not geeing himself up, he's geeing somebody else up.

He's one of those flankers who likes the surfing thing and hanging out at the beach. Razor takes a bit of pride in his appearance, but you would never call him vain, because he laughs at himself and never takes any offence at what might be said.

Razor's doing a course in sports management, and he seems to throw himself into that like he does his football. It's like, 'Yeah, let's go study!'

He throws himself fully into the game right from the first minute, just like he does in life. He holds nothing back. Razor's everywhere during a game.

The one thing that Razor battles with is stepping off both feet. He can go off one, but not the other.

When he played for New Zealand A against the All Blacks in Christchurch in '99, he made a big break down the sideline and went to step one of the guys. He managed to pull off his usual big sidestep, then stepped straight into the tackler.

Watching the game later on TV, you see play develop from the tackle, then a ruck and then a scrum being called. You see the guys packing down getting ready to scrum, and in the background you can see Razor practising his sidestep!

A great guy, very proud to be an All Black. He was very nervous before the World Cup squad was announced. He doesn't do that by halves either. He was as jumpy as you could get before the names were out.

His parents are Mo and Jo. Mo's the big fireman and Jo's his mum. Some of the guys got a bit confused when he first mentioned them, because we thought it was his Mojo he was talking about. But it had nothing to do with Austin Powers.

The one thing that Razor hates is being called 'François'. He doesn't like people saying that he looks like Pienaar, although we reckon it took a while for Canterbury people to realise that we didn't have the ex-South African captain playing off the side of the scrum for us.

JOHN HART used to lean on things when he was talking to the team. He'd pull up a chair and lean on the back, resting his hands on a table.

At the first meeting in '99, at the SAS camp, Harty pulled a table up. He was right into his speech about how tough it was going to be when the whole thing collapsed. He went right to the floor.

Coming on top of '98, when it hadn't gone well, with a big year ahead, nobody wanted to put a foot wrong. So the heads went down, a few guys looked sideways, but only one person laughed, Jane Dent. She was then our media liaison person. She killed herself. We figured that she must have had a contract!

He has a lot of wee idiosyncrasies that would make it quite easy to imitate, should anyone choose to do so . . . which, of course, none of us ever did.

For example, he was quite famous in the team for suddenly breaking into song. Jonah would have put on *Don't Go Breaking My Heart* and from the front of the bus you'd hear this voice just going for it – it would be Harty.

There must have been a lot of times when he had a song running through his mind, because often before training started, when you were just putting your boots on, he'd casually wander by humming away.

He eventually got a more durable watch than the one he had back in '98. Then, he used to be really hammering a point home in a team talk, smacking his fist into his palm, and the watch would come loose and be flapping away beside his hand. Mind you, he didn't miss a beat. He'd keep talking while he was doing the strap back up again.

PETER SLOANE prides himself on being a forward. At a training, if he's running the forwards, and the backs come too close he says, 'Get out of the way you little lizards, or you'll get crushed.'

He's never too stern to have a joke with. 'Sloaney' has the ability to still look serious when he looks at you, and somehow let you know from his expression that he's got the joke and enjoyed it.

Norm Maxwell calls Sloaney 'Without Fail'. Taxi reckons that, without fail, if Sloaney is asked to speak he'll say, 'No, I've got nothing, but all I want to say is . . .' and then he'll start off. When he was with the All Blacks, Harty would ask if he had anything, and Sloaney would go, 'No, not really Harty. I just think we need to get. . . .'

Normy's sitting there going, 'Without fail mate, without fail'. **Colin Meads was a bit like that when he was the All Black manager. Pinetree would say, 'I've got nothing really, but I just want to say, we've never lost to these pricks, and by gee I don't want to see. . . .'** So Sloaney is Without Fail. We'd just like to emphasise, Sloaney, that it was Norm Maxwell who said that.

Sloaney loves his hard school values and attitudes. We all knew that he was a really good listener, who would always be there for you. Sloaney has been through such a lot himself. He defeated cancer, which is the huge one.

GORDON HUNTER is a fantastic guy, a really good joker, who you have to concentrate hard on when he's talking to you. Almost every time he'll come out with a real gem.

Guys really respond well to him. There's a great story the Otago players tell about 1994, when Otago played the Springboks. Apparently the first provincial team to beat them was going to get the mounted Springbok head.

They got to the ground and 'Gordie' went in to have the team talk. He walked in with a hammer and a nail, hammered the nail into the wall and walked out again!

With the All Blacks, Harty was once talking in Christchurch before we played the Springboks. He was saying how clever the Springboks were, and how they got a lot of information on whoever they were playing. How they have informants everywhere. It was pretty serious stuff.

Gordie was sitting down the back next to a couple of boxes. He gives them a big 'whack' and says, 'No bugs here!'

In 1998 there was some criticism that we had too many voices, but that wasn't actually the case. Gordie wasn't talking to the team a lot, so it was, at most, two or three voices, and they were all moving in the same direction.

Gordie is a good rooster to have around. He's a good team man, and he does a lot of work behind the scenes as a selector.

PHOTOSPORT

Gordie Hunter – a top bloke who can always be relied upon to come out with a real gem.

Justin: Throughout 1999 Gordie helped me out a lot. When he thought he needed to give me a call, when things weren't going that well, and the pressure was going on, he'd tell me not to listen to any of the crap that was being said out there. He told me what the selectors wanted from me, what they were looking for, and to stay positive. He does that for players, which is bloody good, and something the public doesn't see.

Mehrts: He's always there as a sounding board, or if you want a yarn. **I also remember in '97 in England, when you'd go out in pretty grey, cold, wet weather he would be the first there to say, 'Do you want someone to come out with you?'**

He'd be standing behind the posts when one went through, and he'd be calling out, 'Yes. A good kick'. That's the sort of attitude that really helps.

RICHARD FRY, or 'Ravishing Rick', was our sponsorship manager, who helped out everybody. We were impressed that while 'Mr Evil' in *Austin Powers* created little 'Mini Me', a shorter version, Mike Banks, as All Black manager, created his own 'Mini Fry'.

'Frybee' was a very good table tennis player, always out there with Christian Cullen. He's a boring player, though, relying on hitting the ball back and waiting for unforced errors.

On the golf course Richard's a gun too, and won a lot of the tournaments – especially when he organised them and determined the handicaps. Some might question that. As well as golf, he's also a good tennis player, but he does struggle with basketball and volleyball, where height is an element. **He's not a huge man, and at an airport when we were waiting for our suitcases, sometimes a toilet bag would be on the carousel, and we'd all yell, 'Frybee, your suitcase is here!'**

He has a host of nicknames. 'Stir Fry', 'Lambs' Fry', 'French Fry' and, of course, 'Ravishing Rick Fry'. He copped a lot of flak from the boys, but he's got such a good sense of humour there was never a problem.

When **DAVID ABERCROMBIE** was our physio, he wore the same sort of small jokes that Frybee did. He's got two sons,

Nigel and Scott, who are about 10 and 13, and when they came to see him, somebody called, 'Hey "Abo", when are your sons finishing varsity?'

Abo had the biggest laugh in the team, and often on the bus there'd be a huge guffaw and it'd be Abo. He's got a keen sense of humour and he's one of those guys you love to catch up with away from the team, because you know you'll have a good evening out.

JOHN MAYHEW, the doctor, is 'Hewie'. When he had his moustache, he bore a striking resemblance to Allan Hewson – if Hewie had been a lock instead of a fullback.

It's a testament to how efficient Doc is that he's been the doctor with the All Blacks for so long. When Doc's on the job, he's on the job! On game day, when you need him, you know you can rely on him. Tell him you need a jab on the day of the game, you can guarantee that he'll be walking around with his needle looking for you.

It'd be fair to say that he enjoys a good laugh. His sense of humour probably tends to the more refined and academic variety. He has some great stories from all the tours he's been on and you enjoy just sitting in his room listening to them.

He's a big family man, with five children, which is living proof that he doesn't spend all of his time tending to injured rugby players.

Doc also churns out a lot of miles running. He's not a smooth, flowing gazelle over the ground, but he's fit and he works hard at it. **He's got massive legs, which makes him an ideal keeper on the odd occasion when we play indoor soccer.**

When we were playing in the Colts **NORM BERRYMAN** was the next big thing, having been a teenage star in the NPC for Northland. He was a big guy then and he was already a household name.

We were just breaking into the scene and here was this guy, larger than life, with an infectious laugh and a love for life.

He balances things out more than you might think. He's not quite as flippant as the impression you might get if you've only seen a brief interview on television.

But he does enjoy what he does. He's a brilliant touch player, a great sevens player, with skills all round, who just gets out there and has a good time.

He was managed brilliantly in the Crusaders by Wayne Smith and Robbie Deans. They were able to get the very best out of him, by encouraging him to be a free spirit, without getting too silly. He was committed to the lot, from the training to the game.

He was comfortable in the environment. He knew the boys respected him for who he was, as well as his ability. In some ways he was able to refine his rugby in Canterbury.

He's got the real knack of not seeming to prepare for a game on the day. **He'll be at training during the week, doing everything he's supposed to and then on the day he'll be fooling around, and then go out and play really well. He seems to get most of his enjoyment from the actual playing.**

Mehrts: He did get nervous once with the Crusaders. In 1998 we played a warm-up tournament in Coolum with Auckland, Queensland and New South Wales.

It was the very first game of the year, against Auckland. All the teams were pretty laid back before the match, to the point where the Aucklanders turned up on pushbikes. For us, too, it was a low key build-up.

But Normy had got so tense that he actually threw up before the game. He was stressed out by it. He's usually really loose, so even a low key build-up for us he found quite tense.

He had a word with Smithy, and he said to him, 'Look, we don't want you feeling like this at all. Just make sure you don't get stuck with serious guys in your build-up. You know Con (Barrell) from Northland and you know Mehrts'. As far as the whole team went, we were probably the most frivolous before a game, and Smithy said to go and hang out with us before a game.

If he could, Con would be eating pies and hot dogs – cruising. So we did that for the rest of the year. Norm and I used to get into a routine where we'd go and walk around the ground before a game, just have a wee wander.

At Jade Stadium it reached a point where, by the time we were going past the bank, they'd be cheering him, and Normy would be waving out and laughing with people in the crowd.

When we got to Durban late in the Super 12, we were walking around about 45 minutes before kickoff and a whole lot of Natal people came flying out and said, 'Do you mind coming up and signing the wall in our corporate box?' It was on the lowest level. **So we hopped over the fence, went up there, had a bit of a yarn and they made a joke about having a drink. Normy's eyes lit up when he saw the fridge.** Then we carried on. So once he knew that the way he built up was accepted, he was fine.

Justin: Not too many people who meet Normy don't get on with him. I really like him. I always found him the same sort of good bloke, wherever you saw him.

When he was in the All Blacks in 1998 he made a remark about there being no 'vibe' in the team. That was so on the mark it wasn't funny, yet some people who read the quote may have wondered what he was on about.

It is important in the team to get the right environment. That ability to be able to loosen up and be yourself is an important part of that.

Basically what he was saying is that he didn't enjoy it, because he wasn't able to be Norm Berryman. He called it the vibe. You could see it when he was around the team.

It was the only time I've been in a team with Norm where he wasn't himself, I don't believe. He tried to loosen up, but he never felt comfortable.

Mehrts: It was a good environment with the Crusaders, but I'd say that Smithy was a little surprised when he first got to know us. While it might have appeared we were a bit flippant, and were taking the mickey the whole week, he trusted us to put in the effort when we were supposed to.

Nothing's sacred. It's been part of our culture for the last

PHOTOSPORT

Normy Berryman in Crusaders mode. He's a guy everyone gets along with.

four to five years. Everyone gets the piss taken out of them something chronic, and there's just a whole lot of laughter. It's quite good, because it brings everybody down to the same level. Everyone gets the same treatment and there's a lot of laughter, which was something Norm enjoyed.

The way Normy played really suited our game. It's all about reacting to what you see happening, rather than going through pre-ordained things so much. A lot of our guys are really good at that.

A lot of the time with Norm, when he had the ball, we had to sit back, run off and just be ready to react to anything. The more we played with him, the better it got.

He can do anything – he has such good vision, and that's why he's such a danger. You've always got to be aware that the ball might suddenly arrive.

Justin: He had injury problems in 2000, and played against the Hurricanes when he wasn't really 100 per cent fit. Then 'Robbo' (Mark Robinson) took his chances.

It was just unfortunate for Norm personally that he had an injury when he did. He had been playing really well. My lasting memory of him in 2000 was him scoring under the posts against Otago.

Mehrts: The odd thing was that this year's Super 12 would probably have suited Norm more than any other. The attack from teams was a lot better, and the way teams develop their attack around a big defensive wall . . . he's ideal for that, just like Tana Umaga.

Essentially, Norm's like Tana with the ball in hand, with probably a few more kicking skills. They're both good decision makers, they can both crack a line themselves, they've both got great steps either way and they can take you forward, and they're both such danger men.

DALLAS SEYMOUR was out of the Canterbury region for a number of years, but when he came back in 2000 he got immediate respect from the guys because of all the things he's done over the years.

... a lot of vitality, and he's good ... ys, who he gets on really easily ... a Maori elder in the team.

... 'Tom Thumb', because when we were ... egions in our Super 12 lead-up we playe... rd cricket. **He's got terrible hands with a tennis ball** ... **son. He's got huge big mitts, and it seemed a bit like he had 10 thumbs.**

Justin: He's a great team man. I watched a video after we'd played Taranaki in the NPC semifinal, and we were battling away and the crowd had gone really quiet.

Play was going on from a ruck and you heard as clear as a bell this voice roaring from the sidelines, 'Come on guys, get excited. Smash someone!' Everyone is sitting there thinking, 'Far out, this is a tough old game'. 'Come on boys', Dallas is up and yelling.

Mehrts: I can remember playing against him in 1992 in a club match, and he was unbelievable. He'd just played in the All Blacks, and I was quite intimidated by him. He was just relentless, almost robotic.

He was good at everything, but because he was so good at sevens he tended to be more involved there, but he's that good a player he could have staked out a good career in the All Blacks if he'd concentrated on fifteens, as an openside flanker.

It's great to have someone with his experience and rugby ability in your team. He just goes hard-out whether he's at No 8, blindside or openside. It'd probably be the same if he was playing at centre.

Both: We all decided a while ago that the prototype of the modern flanker was Scott Robertson. The body type, the speed – all of it being developed by our trainer, 'Mossy' (Mike Anthony). We were going to mould players into perfect flankers.

So Razor and Reuben went along with it, the idea that we'd see these rugby machines for the next century. So they became P1 and P2, and then that pretty boy from Harbour, Ron Cribb, turned up and they reluctantly let him be P3.

So it was a bit of a shock to the system when Dallas came back, because he wasn't quite as young as the rest of them. So they debated for a while whether they should call him a prototype, but they got a bit of a ribbing from the rest of the boys, saying that Dallas was probably the original prototype, so they grudgingly let him in as P4.

If any one of them wins the tackling award they get one of the prototypes to award to another prototype. It just makes everyone sick.

RON CRIBB AND TROY FLAVELL: Where do you start? The twins. Good jokers who have knocked round together for years.

Cribby enjoyed the rugby down here, but perhaps some of the pace of life in Christchurch was a bit slow for his liking. He's a man who loves the Auckland life, living it in the fast lane.

Justin: Some of the clothes he turned up in made a few of the boys put their heads down. **The first few times it was, 'What the hell's he wearing?' Sort of alternative, trendy stuff: wide grey flares, sparkly shirts – Doug Howlett style.**

Then Toddy walks in wearing his grey, zip-up shoes or cowboy boots and blue denim shirts and goes, 'What the hell's going on here?'

Mehrts: He's got everything on the field. He's big, he's strong, he's fast, and he's got a good attitude.

Justin: He's always had the ability. In the Crusaders he played that Zinny type of No 8 game. He had the chance to express his skills and use what he had, which is why he came on so quickly – from not wanted in the Blues to playing for the All Blacks.

Mehrts: I remember when Cribby did his first interview after he became an All Black. He said that in his first test he just wanted to make sure he got through the game without letting anyone down, or making too many mistakes, and after that he wanted to express himself. I reckon old All Black No 8s would

PETER BUSH

Ron Cribb shows off his skills for the All Blacks against Scotland early in the international season.

PETER BUSH

Troy Flavell – the other twin – settles a disagreement with the Springboks during the 2000 Tri-Nations.

have been horrified. The idea of a No 8 wanting to express himself isn't in the older books.

Both: Cribby's good value, with a good sense of humour, too. **He and 'Flavs' would have a 'Westie' section of a court session, where they'd go over some of their escapades when they were in their youth in the hard streets of West Auckland.**

It was almost like a rap. They'd both stand up, swaying away, talking like rappers and talking about how they pinched fish hooks and stuff. It was very funny.

Wherever you go there'd be a Cribb senior. Jim Cribb used to come down quite a bit to see his son play, and Jim's got at least two or three brothers scattered around the country. **So everywhere you went they'd be Cribby Junior, because he looks like his dad, who was Cribb Senior, and there were always other seniors as well.**

TODD BLACKADDER: Everybody knows how good a captain he is. He's got his own style. Before Toddy, captains used to have to have their own room, but he'd rather have one of the younger captains in his room, making cups of tea for him.

You'd look in Toddy's room and there he'd be, lying on his bed, sipping out of a cup of tea while the young guy is running around all the other rooms looking for more tea bags, and more biscuits.

Mehrts: I was rooming with him once and I woke up to the sound of this massive blast from the bed across the room, and you could sense the smile in his voice when he said, 'Is the jug on Priscilla?'

Both: Everyone likes him and he has the ability to laugh at himself, too. He doesn't get ribbed a lot, other than about the size of his butt. You just don't feel like getting stuck into him, really.

He never talks down to people at all. You just know that he's fully in behind everything; his heart and soul are always in it, and he's willing to do as much as everyone else put together to achieve the aim.

PETER BUSH

Toddy's just Toddy. A top player and a top captain who never talks down to anyone.

He speaks very plainly, he doesn't go on a lot. He keeps it very simple, which is the way the game should be.

Mehrts: My favourite moment from Todd was in a game where there'd been a bit of a dust-up and the referee said to Todd, go back and tell your players to cool it down.

We were all standing around, behind our own goal-line, knowing that Toddy's been told to come and tell us to cut the crap out.

So Toddy comes back and all the players come in. We all know exactly what he's supposed to say to us and he goes, 'They don't bloody score here!' That's it.

Justin: One of his classic decisions was in the game in Pretoria last year when it was incredibly hot. We were behind going into injury time and we had to win it to stay in with a chance of making the semifinals.

We got a scrum on their 22m and we were all coming to the scrum. I sort of looked at Toddy for a bit of advice. I can picture it now. We've joked about it since. We're all tired and I turned to our leader of men – the sweat fair hosing off him. His jersey's hanging out, he's sucking in air and he says to me, 'Just bloody do something!' Then he buries his head in the scrum. Classic.

I thought, hell, we'd better go for a drop kick.

Mehrts: And I didn't want to. I thought they'd all expect the drop kick, so I wanted Cribby to run off from No 8. They'd follow him and we'd sweep blind and catch them on the hop. In the end Justin didn't hear me and I started moving to where I shouldn't have been. I had to go back to grab the ball. It turned out to be the best thing we could have done.

Both: Toddy sets the general pattern and he'll make the decisions on shots at goal, but it's not part of the job of a captain in the forwards to call the moves in the backs. **Mind you, if we're hard on defence and the backs start to move it around a bit, you'll hear this big roar, 'Just kick the bloody thing down there!'**

You'll see him with all types of people and he sincerely

listens to them. He doesn't just nod them off. He'll be polite and treat them like their opinion is the most important one in the world.

The older generation really love him, possibly because of his grey hair, but he's always being given teddy bears, cakes . . . all sorts of things.

He's always been a bit of a father figure in teams. With young guys he comes up with that great big wooden paw and chucks it on the back, 'Are you alright mate?'

Even before he was captain of the All Blacks he was very well liked everywhere he went and well respected by other international players. It was quite interesting during the Super 12 that guys in Australia and South African would say, 'Do you think Toddy's going to be the All Black captain? He should get it.'

He just has that effect on people – from people seeing how he goes out and gives it everything, every time he plays.

Toddy basically wears his heart on his sleeve, he doesn't try to be anything he's not, and people get what they see. People who haven't even met him feel they know him pretty well. Essentially they do, because he is exactly what he comes across as.

There's a dignity about guys like Toddy and Brian Lochore. Around guys like them you don't even feel like talking too loudly.

SEAN FITZPATRICK: Mehrts: He was one player who always managed to balance things really well. **It may have been just because he was a legend, and I was new to the team, but in 1995 I always got the impression he managed to slip into the corporate thing, and back into the playing role, very well.**

He was serious when he needed to be, when he was in effect one of the management team, but then was very much one of the guys when he was with the team.

We didn't hold too much back when Marshy and I were playing cards with him. He gives that big laugh, 'Ha, ha, ha, HAH'. To this day he'll occasionally leaves messages on the

PHOTOSPORT

**Sean Fitzpatrick – very hard and very competitive. Fitzy was the
ultimate professional.**

answerphone that are simply just that laugh.

He was a guy I'd watched for eight years at the pinnacle, and to then play alongside him was a huge buzz. He was very hard and very competitive. At training he'd clip a guy, not out of any malice, but just to make sure they were hard and ready for the job.

Justin: All those guys were intensely competitive from that Auckland team of the 'Fitzy' and Zinzan Brooke era. It was good for us as younger players to be in there with guys who were so intensely focused on their jobs in the team, and taking training so seriously.

They made you realise what a big step up it was to become an All Black, but then they'd come and sit around over cards with you.

If we were playing cricket in a hotel corridor, they'd come along and join in. It wasn't the sort of thing that, when I wasn't in the All Blacks, I would have ever imagined a Sean Fitzpatrick or a Zinzan Brooke doing.

Mehrts: They were a lot more normal than some people might have thought. When I was at school, growing up in Canterbury, we hated Brooke, Fitzpatrick, Bernie McCahill, and Mark Carter. To be honest, though, I look back now and they're four of the top jokers you could ever meet.

I quite liked the fact that they actually got stuck in with a genuine dislike about Canterbury. **They got stuck back into us, didn't just treat us patronisingly, like, 'We're from Auckland and we don't give a stuff about anyone else.'**

MIKE BREWER: He was probably more intense than Fitzy, and he was a dominant figure at training. He could enjoy a good laugh, but we probably didn't have him on as much as we did Fitzy.

Mehrts: I enjoyed seeing him one night flare up when he was the captain of the Canterbury team. I'd been out on the juice with Graeme Bachop, Aaron Flynn and Angus Gardiner.

We rocked back in at about three o'clock and rolled into 'Bruiser's' room. So Angus and I, being youngsters, just sat on the end of the bed, but Graeme and Aaron started to niggle up Bruiser a bit. He'd been asleep, and we'd woken him up, but he was fine.

Then they started to niggle him up a bit too much, so he leaps out of bed, naked, and starts taking really big swings at 'Grim' and 'Oogie'. He's saying, 'Well, put your money where your mouth is.'

Angus and I are just sitting there, scared to death, and there's a real ding dong battle for five minutes. Both halfbacks have got hold of him – Oogie around his torso and Grim's got him in a headlock, saying, 'Bruiser, I could break your neck here, just settle down.'

I was pretty impressed. Mike had just leapt into it without a moment's hesitation.

ZINZAN BROOKE: We used to call him 'Easter Island', because he's got a very big head. You certainly know when he's in the room.

Justin: Mehrts knew him before I did, but when I did get into the All Blacks with 'Zinny' in 1995 I was crapping myself about meeting him.

I'd only just moved up to Christchurch and to suddenly be hanging out with Zinny, Fitzy, Michael Jones, it was all a bit much.

We assembled at the Poenamo Hotel in Takapuna and they read out the rooming list. **I was really hoping I'd be with Mehrts, or Taine, someone I knew. They went, 'Justin Marshall/Zinzan Brooke'. I was horrified.**

I grabbed my bags and took them up to the room. He was lying on the big double bed. I came in and he sort of smiled and said, 'G'day'. I said, 'How are you going Zinny'. No, I think I said Zinzan.

His bags were sort of sitting on my bed. So I said, 'Ah, I'll just put my bags by your bags, grab a pillow and lie down here on the floor, eh. Is that alright?'

He says, 'Aw, no mate, it's okay'. He grabbed his bags, and straight away it was as good as gold. He started asking

PHOTOSPORT

The one and only Zinny Brooke – he was a rock, he was an island (an Easter Island).

questions, because I couldn't really think of anything to talk about. From then on it was brilliant.

We roomed together a lot because that's what they tend to do it with guys who are playing close together on the field.

He's a guy who will find something to compete over everywhere. I think it was in Sydney, I came into the room and I drained a bottle of water and put the empty plastic bottle on top of the television.

Zinny was lying back on his bed watching TV, and he had a bottle of water as well. He finished it and then, whack, he fired it at the TV, trying to knock my water bottle off.

Then he reaches down and grabs another bottle so he can try again. I grab another bottle too, and next thing we're chopping through these bottles of water, and biffing them at the empty bottle, trying to beat each other.

We couldn't get it until we were about four or five bottles down. He made up rules, like he always does. You had to lie back on the bed, you weren't allowed to wind up for a decent shot.

Kids, don't try this at home. Zinny was the first one to get up feeling really very ill, totally bloated, over-hydrated.

We ended up taking turns sitting on the toilet with water coming out everywhere.

Mehrts: There's a history of Brooke versus Marshall drinking contests. In South Africa in 1996 we were in the team room and Justin got up to get a Coke. Zinny had one too. Suddenly he noticed what Justin was drinking and started slugging down bigger and bigger gulps, getting the Coke down.

Anywhere you went with Zinny and his mates there'd be a game on. If you were sitting around for a couple of minutes for a team meeting, they'd have a coin out and would be rolling it to see who could get it closest to a wall.

Olo Brown would join in, and he'd be setting rules, too. As an accountant, Olo wasn't unaccustomed to living by a set of rules. They'd all be in there, making up the rules, deciding who would win what for a victory.

We were invited to a casino once. We all got about a $50 chip each. Straight away the boys started playing 'rock, paper, scissors' against each other and I think Zinny ended up with about 15 chips before he'd even gambled at the casino.

Justin: He was sour if he lost, though. **A real bad loser. I've seen him throw a cricket bat in a corridor.**

Mehrts: I respect that. I'm a bad loser, too.

Justin: Zinny was always working out a whole bunch of moves. He'd wake you up to tell you, 'How do you think this would go, Marshy?' I'd say, 'Yeah, I reckon that'd work Zinny.'

Mehrts: In 1993 the All Blacks were playing the Lions and Anthony Lawry and I were a couple of the local guys who went out to be cannon fodder for the All Blacks at training.

We were holding a tackle bag and all Zinny did was come off the back of a scrum, take about four or five steps, and then whack into the bag. The two of us just flew back about four or five metres. The power and his hard-nosed approach were just awesome.

I first met Zinny at the start of the '95 season. I had missed a lot of the trials before the World Cup with a deep bruise in my thigh, but I came back to play in the game in Hamilton for the Harlequins, where Zinny got his famous Achilles injury. He was really scared that he was going to miss the World Cup.

I was rooming with Zinny, and what I remember vividly about the night after the game was that every two-and-a-half hours I'd wake up and Zinny and Alison, who's now his wife, were icing Zinny's leg.

It was a phenomenal example of how committed he was. I'd never encountered that sort of thing before, because I'd never had a serious injury. The dedication he showed to getting it healed, and then the fact he did get through to the World Cup, was astonishing.

Justin: I count my lucky stars that I came along when I did. Playing outside Zinny, and inside Mehrts, what could you really do wrong? The abilities that Zinny had to see what was happening, and to adjust and react to it, were remarkable.

PETER BUSH

Leon MacDonald is a player who can slot in anywhere. He's also a player who can turn his hand to most other sports.

Mehrts: To even train with guys like Zinny, Fitzy and Olo Brown was something special.

LEON MACDONALD: His name in the team is 'Rangi', and it comes from the Maori boy in *Footrot Flats*, the one who's hard as nails and tackles like a maniac on the footie field. Apparently it started back when he was a kid growing up in Marlborough.

When he first came to Canterbury as a teenager he was at fullback in the 1997 NPC final against Counties, and he smoked George Laupepe – who's a big unit – and then stopped Joeli Vidiri head on.

He can play anywhere because he's so fast. He doesn't look as quick as what he really is. He and Ben Blair would be about the same pace.

If Leon puts his head back when he runs, the ears might

slow him down a little bit, but with a tail wind behind him he's unbeatable. It's like having the spinnaker out.

He never seems to be as young as he actually is. He's been around for years. Leon can play anything – golf, cricket, probably tennis if he put his mind to it. He's one of our regular golf players.

MARK ROBINSON: More spinnakers in the ear department. We've always felt that you could put MacDonald, Mayerhofler and Robinson side by side and there wouldn't be a single gap in the backline.

Amongst the rugby crowd he's a very cerebral guy, quite quiet, almost pensive, but he reads the game really well.

The great thing about him at centre is that if he makes a break he always looks out. The rule always was that you make the break, then you feed. A lot of guys now tend to make the break and then look inside.

Mehrts: His first game for the Crusaders was in 2000 in a build-up match in Sydney. It was hosing down, and it was just astounding to me how he could read the play.

I was changing direction all the time, much to Justin's annoyance, and wherever I went Robbo was there ready to take the pass . . . and the gap.

You can see that he's a guy who's thought things through and worked hard at making it happen.

Both: Naturally he gets heaps about having been at Cambridge University, just as everyone in the team gets heaps about whatever they've done.

He did make a couple of bad mistakes early on. He said, 'Good morning chaps' one day. That opened the field of attack up a bit.

Then there was the time when we were in the changing room after a Canterbury game. We always go around the room and say something – if someone's had a blazer game, let's say, or any thoughts on the match.

Robbo got up and said, 'Yes, congratulations to everyone on their respective achievements'. Uproar. From then on, every time there's a need for it, someone else will congratulate people for their respective achievements.

MARK MAYERHOFLER: It'd take hours to really convey the admiration everyone has for 'Bubs'.

He's a great team man, but it's a bit hard to talk about him because everybody just has praise for him, and he's such a nice bloke.

It's just a measure of the guy that if he has anything to say then you can hear a pin drop. **Genuinely the best bloke and the hardest worker you could ever meet. He's just been our rock for the last five or six years.**

Justin: He was very unlucky to be injured when he was. He could have had a lot to offer still to the All Blacks.

Mehrts: I was just rapt for him when he did make the All Blacks, because while everybody puts in the work, Bubs does that more so than anyone. His commitment on and off the field is amazing – everyone just loves the guy.

WAYNE SMITH is pretty much everything you could want in a coach. He just loves the All Blacks and what they stand for. He puts everything into it.

If people could see how he operates they'd be very encouraged. He has passion for the game and the team, great desire and he leaves no stone unturned to get it right.

When it means that much to you, he can get pretty tense towards the end of the week when a game's due. It's almost a standing joke with us that on the day before a game he'll just sidle up to you and murmur something like, 'Have you thought about maybe just popping it up behind their wingers, perhaps just a little bit higher?' Just little fine tuning things that have been covered during the week.

He is a coach who'll really listen to the players. If Toddy goes to him and says, 'Look, the boys are having too many meetings this week', then Smithy will just chop them.

He's quite happy to take a back seat to manager Andrew Martin in everything except the coaching. Smithy can concentrate on that, and let Andrew run the rest.

Mehrts: I think the first year with the Crusaders was quite a growing year for Smithy and for us. At the time he was reasonably technical and scientific too, which was probably a result of having coached in Italy, at Benetton, where he had to get the technical aspects of the game right.

It might also have come from his days coaching sevens, which at the time was a developing sport, and he was always analysing his own methods.

So in the first year of the Crusaders, I think he developed a balance, and from then on everything clicked. Not that being so scientific in the first year was necessarily a bad thing. We did jump from being last in Super 12 to sixth place.

Both: He's not a technocrat. **He's always said with the computer work and stats that he uses that it's not the be all and end all. It's just an indication.**

Sometimes guys can't remember their own game that well, and the computer analysis is just a method for a player to be able to go back and look, to see exactly what happened. You can use it to find and correct specific errors that are cropping up.

He likes guys to think for themselves. He's always been one to encourage guys to ask questions, because he must feel that at least a player is concentrating on his game.

Smithy's got a natural respect for players and his whole aim is just to get the best out of them. It's easy when you're talking to Smithy, knowing that he has confidence in you. He talks pretty much on an equal level.

When it's time to be serious he does it in a very professional way and keeps things calm and simple, so everyone can take it on board.

He has a good sense of humour about himself. We have him on about his Afro hairdo, and he can laugh about that. He used to get called 'Mahoney', because we reckon he looks like Steve Guttenberg, who played Mahoney in those *Police Academy* **movies.**

When he was coaching with Peter Sloane, that meant, of course, that Sloaney was 'Tackleberry', the huge cop

PETER BUSH

Patrolman 'Mahoney' Smith watches over an All Black training session.

obsessed with guns in *Police Academy*.

He is a very competitive man, whether it's cricket, or touch, or tennis, or squash. Certainly if you're playing doubles in tennis with him, he doesn't hesitate to make sure you're playing up to your best standards.

TONY GILBERT is a case of what you see is very much what you get. People warm to the 'Big Tee' really easily.

All the Otago boys had always raved about him, and that helps a guy when people like Hatchet Oliver have had a lot of time for him.

Tony's straight up, straight talking and in many ways has similar views on coaching to Smithy. They want the simple things done well, and don't like to complicate the issue. They see rugby as a simple game if the basic things are done properly.

They work well together. Sometimes Smithy will get into the techniques of what's wanted, and it won't be rocket science, but it will be technical. **Then Tony will get up and say, 'Keep that in mind forwards, but at the end of the day we just need to front up and knock some bastards over.'**

There's no clash of egos at all between the two. Some of us wondered when they were appointed whether two guys who had been in charge of their own teams would work easily together, but because of their personalities, there's never been any hint of a problem.

Mehrts: We've got a website, where guys can log in and get their training schedules and things like that. For the first couple of months there were flurries of e-mails and, being dubbed 'e-Mehrtens' by the boys, I was flat out sending messages.

Big Tee had sent a couple of messages on the site and I started calling him 'Medium Tee' for some reason. Straight away there was a message for me saying, 'Any time you're ready Mehrts, bring it on. I'm waiting for you.'

He can banter as well as anyone, but Tony is a bit like Toddy in that he's one guy that for some reason you don't want to take the piss out of too much.

PETER BUSH

**Andrew 'The Colonel' Martin
with a young supporter.**

ANDREW MARTIN is a man who has obviously been very focused all his working life in the Army, and brings that to the All Black manager's position.

It's quite funny when he relaxes and you hear this huge booming laugh at team sessions.

Once at a team session the boys all wanted Army stories, tales of conflict, so 'The Colonel' talked about a parachute drop.

He was miming what happens while the parachute is coming down, hopping around on one leg, making 'whooshing' sounds. **It just looked hilarious, a grown man in his position with his big frame doing the parachute dance.**

We'd first met him when we did the SAS camp in 1999 and so our first experience of him was as this figure of great authority in the Army who put us all through torture.

When we first met him we wondered what we might strike, but the guys warmed to him when we saw how passionate he was about the team, and how much effort he threw at it.

Mehrts: We have something in common I discovered. **We both hate being called 'Andy'. So naturally the time had to come when he handed me something, and I casually went, 'Thanks very much Andy.'**

He just flared the eyes a bit, and that was enough. It's a bit of a joke for us now. Every now and then we chuck the Andy call at one another.

Both: People might be genuinely surprised at the level of commitment there is in the All Black camp, from the management through to all the players.

GILBERT ENOKA: The assistant manager of the All Blacks. The best way to describe Gilbert is that he's a good guy.

People have tended to paint Gilbert as some sort of mental guru for the team, which might imply some sort of airy fairy psychological stuff.

At the end of the day he's actually a switched on guy, who likes to keep things simple. For example, when he works with the Crusaders, he's the one at the start of the season who takes notes during our planning sessions.

He's great at being able to collate that so that we can set goals, help keep our focus and stay on course through the season.

His organising skills are excellent behind the scenes, which is how he likes to keep it.

There wouldn't be a player in the All Blacks who would have a bad word to say about Gilbert. He's the easiest guy to have a yarn to, who has a real knack of putting things into perspective.

Mehrts: For me, I felt that I needed to get a bit more organised. I felt that in our game reviews I needed a way where I could gauge my progress. He helped with that, and with organising my week leading into a game.

DOUG HOWLETT: Has always been a smart player, with lots of gas and courage, who always makes the right decisions.

He cops a bit of flak, whether it's the fact that he has hair like Wayne Smith, or that he looks like Ron Cribb, or that he may be a Greek soccer player masquerading as an All Black.

There have been suggestions that he plays for Panathinaikos in the European soccer league, and that he really should be wearing a gold medallion to go with his heritage.

He actually feels he is one of the fashion leaders in the team. We don't know if he's really a man about town in Auckland, but he seems to know the scene.

Dougie's a fantastic player and it was great to see him getting

Dougie Howlett does the autograph thing. Is he really a Greek soccer player masquerading as an All Black?

tries in all the games on tour. Mind you, you'd expect a lot of tries from a man who scored a try with his first touch of the ball in a test. (Howlett scored against Tonga within a minute of coming onto the field.)

BRUCE REIHANA: 'Bruiser' is a really interesting guy, who is pretty quiet, which you might not anticipate from someone who's so ebullient on the field.

People would be pleased to see how committed, and willing, players like Bruiser and Dougie Howlett are.

Inside the team there's a pretty free way of dealing with each other, which if you're all mates is fine, and there's always a bit of gyp going backwards and forwards, which Bruiser is always relaxed about.

GORDON SLATER is a really good bloke who always does more than he's asked in every single way.

PETER BUSH

Jason O'Halloran shows off his latest hairdo. It does pale, however, against Mehrts' well coiffeured locks.

He goes back a long way with Toddy. They were both in the New Zealand Colts in 1991 and 1992, when they beat the Aussies both years.

Of course Gordon gets heaps about the cows. Daryl Gibson was the 'info' man in France and Italy, and somehow Daryl was able to get a reference into every report. **He'd say, 'A real highlight for Gordy yesterday was seeing a French charolais herd from the bus when we were driving to training.'**

JASON O'HALLORAN is a player it was great to see getting a crack at the All Blacks after being respected by the guys for consistently performing year after year.

The whole team felt enormously for him when he had the tragedy of his mother dying while we were in Japan. It was tough to see Jason go. Equally, though, it was great to see him when he was able to rejoin the tour.

Mehrts: I'd be the last one to be able to throw rocks at anyone's running style – Marshy is always giving me heaps about mine. But I was always getting into Jason about the way he shuffles when he runs. I reckon he looks like he's got no hamstrings. So that was one area of contention.

Then there's the fact that Jason, like me, has had more than his fair share of terrible hair days, that we're the same age, and that we're both pale as hell. It means it's easy for me to get into him, because I'm really looking at myself.

Justin On Mehrts

In the minds of rugby fans they're an on-field duo who fit, whether it's for Canterbury or the All Blacks. They're also good friends, a relationship that goes back to teenaged years. So how did a boy from Mataura in Southland, who in the summer was a demon fast bowler, and a kid from Christchurch, who was a top flight junior tennis player, end up as mates and team-mates? **JUSTIN MARSHALL** gives his views on the friendship.

We played against each other in age teams, but we didn't really know who the other guy was. He played for Canterbury and I was playing for Southland.

We played together for the first time in the New Zealand under-19 team, coached by Vance Stewart, who would eventually coach us for Canterbury and the Crusaders.

The under-19 team did an internal tour of New Zealand, starting in Wellington, after the Colts trial. Then we made our way down the country, through Nelson, Blenheim, Timaru, and then on to Dunedin, where we played the Australian under-19s . . . and where I met up with George Gregan for the first time. So with Mehrts and George I met up with two smarties for the price of one!

For me, that team was something I was really taken aback

by. Coming from down south I thought that just going to the South Island tournaments was pretty neat. Then I got to go to the Colts trials and then the under-19s at the police college.

There were a lot of friendships formed in that under-19 side. There were guys like Norm Berryman, Tabai Matson, Taine Randell, and Mehrts. There were a lot of players who went a lot further in the game.

There was never anything really dramatic about how Mehrts and I clicked. We just seemed to get on reasonably well from the start.

In many ways Mehrts hasn't really changed from when he was a teenager. I mean he still looks like a kid, doesn't he? I reckon he was born with that haircut.

I do know that when we first knew each other I kept thinking, 'Gee, he talks a lot!' First-fives and halfbacks are supposed to talk a lot, but I found I was being out-talked by this guy, which isn't supposed to happen.

I'm a pretty loud person at the best of times, but Mehrts is really hyperactive. He's always all go, and if anything's happening, he's amongst it right away.

With his finely tuned sense of humour, he's pretty quick, so if there's something going on, he's in on the joke. He chimes in with something that will sometimes go whoosh right past the wicketkeeper. Let's face it, we're not all as intelligent as he is, and when he's being really clever, some of us miss out on what's going on.

Mehrts is someone who just never seems to slow down. He's a bit of a night owl, too. On tour he's a midnight sort of person, and then you see him in the morning he's all go again. I don't know where he gets his energy from. Perhaps it's the Coca-Cola, or the cakes of chocolate he monsters. It's not often that you go round to Mehrts' place and don't see a big bag of M and Ms in the pantry.

I moved to Canterbury for the 1995 season. Vance Stewart was the coach. I'd been with him in the under-19 team, with some of the Canterbury boys, who he'd taken through. Mehrts

PETER BUSH

Saluting his adoring fans, Mehrts heads back to the changing sheds after another tough day on the training field.

and Tabs, in particular, had really stepped up for him for Canterbury.

It's always seemed to me that it was basically through Mehrts that I got the chance to play for Canterbury. It was really through Mehrts that I expressed the wish that if I got the chance to play for Canterbury, I'd be really thrilled. I didn't say it to Vance directly, but I told Mehrts exactly how I felt and how I'd love the chance to advance my rugby in Canterbury. **Whether Mehrts had a whisper in Vance's ear or not I'm not sure, but I do know that the word came back to me that Canterbury would be interested in giving me a shot.**

Going to Mehrts' club, Old Boys, was all part of my devious master plan. I looked at it closely. Mehrts was the incumbent Canterbury first-five and I figured it couldn't do me any harm to get some time in at Old Boys with him and try to build up a combination.

But the master plan didn't work at all. He got selected for the All Blacks and was gone! I went to Old Boys and he went to the World Cup and played all those test matches, while I was back in Christchurch.

The funny thing is there were two Justin Marshalls in the Old Boys team, the flanker and myself. With our names being pretty close together in the programme, and nobody knowing who I was, I think there was some real confusion at the start of '95.

To be honest I was really thrilled for Mehrts when he made the All Blacks and, as it turned out, it was actually a good thing for me, too. Seeing him there started me thinking that if I worked really hard, I could have a chance, just as he had.

It was a great motivation for me. Not in a cocky way, not thinking, 'Well, if he can do it, so can I', but an inspiration to see how far I could take this game of rugby.

I was fortunate enough to make the Canterbury side and when Mehrts came back from the World Cup we were not only playing the NPC together, but Canterbury also held the Ranfurly Shield.

It was a huge step up for me. I'd gone from playing second

division rugby, to Ranfurly Shield rugby, which is even more intense than first division NPC. We were playing in front of massive crowds at Lancaster Park and I was absolutely thrilled to be involved.

I was very lucky the way things worked out for me. I was really never expecting to be anywhere near contention for the All Blacks. I thought I'd need to prove myself for at least a couple of seasons before I was even considered.

But I guess there was a shortage of halfbacks, and in the situation I was in, there was a lot of attention because of the television coverage of the shield games – not to mention the fact I was playing in a bloody good side.

Things don't just happen and there was a lot of work to do myself, but playing with so many All Blacks, in such high profile games, was just about perfect if you were a young player trying to make an impact.

Mehrts helped me out a hell of a lot during that season, which I really appreciated.

At the end of the year I was selected for the All Blacks to tour Italy and France. I was just a new kid on the block, but from the under-19 team there was Mehrts, Tabs, Taine, Jeff Wilson, and myself, all together again.

The real shame was that Mehrts got injured in the very first game, in Italy. We were all young guys, and Mehrts was our boss on the laundry committee. Taine and I became his little servants.

I got the second test on that tour and Simon Culhane was Mehrts' replacement, which was the best possible thing for me, because I'd played a lot with Simon for Southland.

We were without Mehrts for most of the Super 12 season while he recovered from the Italian injury.

Then we went to South Africa with the All Blacks and he injured his knee at training. **He's a shocker with those injuries. He only got to play the first and the fourth tests over there. Simon Culhane played the rest.**

It does help if you're used to playing with one guy on a

regular basis. With Mehrts, because I've played with him so much, you know that his decision is going to be the right one and that if it's not, he's a good enough player to get himself out of trouble.

I think even more so it's a lot of planning on the field, calling the shots, and if you've got people who are familiar with each other, you know what the other's likely to want to do in certain situations. It just makes it so much easier. You're not trying to be the dominator because you know that what he wants is what he's likely to get. With somebody you don't know as well, you're possibly not sure if they're comfortable with what's happening.

There's also a situation where he'll call something, and I'll say, 'No, I don't want to do that'. **Let's remember that Mehrts is a dummy-spitting first-five, and if he's adamant about something, you've got to be pretty good to convince him otherwise.** So for me just to say, 'no', and for him to maybe be a little upset about it, but to accept it, is an understanding that's important.

At a scrum call, the forwards want to know what's happening – which side the ball's going as they're forming up. You've got to look at each other and make a call. You haven't time to argue about it, throw the ball down, hands on hips, spit the mouthguard out, and say, 'What?'

You've got to have confidence in each other in what you're calling – and that the call is right. That doesn't come straight away. You're going to have disagreements. **Mehrts and I still have them. After the game we'll talk about it, and there are no recriminations.**

We have all sorts of code names for various moves. It might be a nickname, or the name of a wrestler. All sorts of funny things. One of our codes in the All Blacks was 'Ul-Haq' because we reckoned that Taine looked and batted like Pakistani cricketer Inzamam-Ul-Haq. Another one is 'Setford', after a pic that well-known photographer Ross Setford once took of Taine with a bit of a teapot look to it.

PETER BUSH

Mehrts takes the running option for the All Blacks during the Tri-Nations series.

It doesn't really matter what the code name is, just as long as it sticks in your mind.

We tend to regroup every year. And although the old favourite coded moves are still there, the defences now are so well drilled that you have to try to come up with something new all the time to attempt to score.

When a move does work, you get a lot of satisfaction from it. You do have some standard stock moves, like a double miss, which has probably been handed down from years and years ago.

Getting back to Mehrts, here are a couple of classic stories.

One's about spitting the dummy. It was before a Crusaders game when Tabai Matson was still playing in Canterbury.

Tabai, me and Daryl Gibson used to play 'claps'. It's just a game where you flick the ball around and you have to clap before you catch it. You stand in a circle and you're allowed to throw dummies. **If you clap when somebody throws you the ball, they've dummied you – and you're out.**

We used to have a series of games and one day Mehrts decided to come and join us. We have our own little set of rules, and the majority rules. If we say you've clapped, then you've clapped. Everybody will jump on the bandwagon, 'Yeah, you clapped, you're out.'

So you can imagine that when Mehrts joined in he got dummied and we said, 'No, you clapped, we heard you, you're out'. 'No I didn't'. 'All three of us heard you, you're out'. 'No, I didn't'. Then he grabbed the ball and told us we were dickheads. 'You can't do this.'

We said, 'Look Mehrts, don't worry about it, you're out. You can come back in when this game's finished'. He said, 'If you want an honesty call, this is a dead set honesty call. I'm not lying. Do you guys know what an honesty call means?'

We all looked at each other and said, 'You're out.'

Then he said, 'Right', and he booted the ball right out of the hotel car park and it bounced across Papanui Rd. He said something like, 'Marshall, you're a bogan from Southland, Matson, you haven't played well in three years, Gibson you're blah, blah, blah'. Then he stormed away up the stairs.

We were all just standing there staring. It was hilarious. He was genuinely wild because he hates people cheating, and he called us cheats and stormed off. We had to go and get the ball – it wrecked our game and then we had to be all brothers in arms in the game that afternoon!

The other story is about a court session in King Country, in 1995 when we still had the Ranfurly Shield. They walloped us and Mike Brewer called a massive big session.

Mehrts was steadily getting a bit of courage out of a glass.

Next to him was Richard Loe, who was just sitting there, being himself. Mehrts just emptied his beer over the top of Loey's head.

Loey jumped up, roaring, and he grabbed Mehrts by the throat, and all of a sudden Mehrts just slumped, out to it. Loey had put him to sleep!

Everybody was going, 'Mehrts, Mehrts'. It was so funny to watch. Mehrts had thought it was so amusing pouring the beer over Loey, and then he got the sleeper hold put on him. Eventually Mehrts woke up. He certainly never tipped any beer on Loey again!

Mehrts and I do socialise, by choice, a fair bit. We're not in each other's pockets, but we do get on so well that we can take that away from a rugby environment and take it somewhere else.

We'll go and watch Canterbury play cricket together, or my wife and I will come in to his place and have dinner with him. He's too lazy to drive out to Sumner, but we'll come in to see him. We do socialise outside rugby when we don't have to.

It was rugby that started our friendship, but it's not that keeping it there and continuing it. We're mates.

Mehrts On Justin

Now it's the turn of the tennis player to evaluate the Mataura Kid.

There aren't too many guys I can personally stomach listening to before a game. To me it's your own time, a time when you build yourself up, look after yourself and trust the other guys are looking after themselves.

Toddy's one I can listen to – or whoever's captain – and every now and then, with Canterbury, someone like Matt Sexton or Stu Loe will say something, and that's fine.

The only other guy I can listen to, and if he wants to say it then I'm 100 per cent behind him, is Justin.

He's one of the few guys that I really respect to be able to pick the pulse of the team and say something that's on the mark. I rate that.

Right from the time he moved to Christchurch in 1995 I knew that he was a leader, and although I missed the Super 12 in 1996 with a knee injury, I know he was playing a leadership role there.

Since then he's always been a leader off the field, at training, and if he's got something to say, guys will shut up and listen.

My first encounter with Justin goes back to the first experience I had of playing in a Canterbury team. It was when

I got picked for the under-18 side for a South Island tournament in 1991, my first year out of school.

We played Southland in the final and won 29–9. Marshall claims ever since that they were on the turps the night before. Yeah, whatever.

In that team they had Jeff Wilson and Justin, and quite a few guys who came through later on. **Justin had played right through for Southland from the under-16s, but I didn't meet him until Vance Stewart picked Justin and me in the South Island under-18 team.**

We played one game at Rugby Park against a Canterbury development team and they gave us a real thumping. But it was a real buzz to play for the South Island. Jeff Wilson, Tabai Matson, Jamie Connelly, quite a few players who had very good senior careers, were in the side.

Justin was the halfback and I was the first-five. In those days we were thrown together for one game and then shot away again. I didn't get to know him that well then.

But the next year Vance was the coach of the New Zealand under-19 team which went to Blenheim, Timaru, and then went to Dunedin and played against the Australian Colts.

We had a hell of a strong team. Taine Randell was in the forwards, and we had Norm Berryman, Tabai Matson, Adrian Cashmore, those sort of guys.

When you look back at Justin then he was a tough kid from Mataura. He'd been in the freezing works and he was pretty worldly as far as working with men goes. He was devastating at age group level, just so hard.

He was really the forerunner of the big, strong New Zealand halfbacks. Before then you had guys like Graeme Bachop and Dave Loveridge, who were quick and skilled, rather than being able to act almost as an extra loose forward at times.

The 1992 tour was where Justin and I started to get to know each other. There were some real characters in the team, and Norm Berryman and Justin would stand out in that regard.

Those two hit it off fantastically. It's sort of an odd thing when you think about it, isn't it? Here was this Maori guy from the far north, although I think Normy's family are actually Tainui from the Waikato, and the redneck from Southland. They got on like a house on fire.

A lot of the jokes that started then still endure, the way we address each other – it all goes back to then.

Justin was never up himself or anything like that, but he was always in the middle of things, as he likes to be.

On the field he stood out as the most abrasive, tough, competitive of the halfbacks. Off the field he hit it off with everyone, a real life and soul guy with a good sense of humour.

By the end of 1994 we'd had two years of Colts rugby. The first year Elton Moncrieff played at halfback and I was at first-five. The next year Justin was at halfback, but Carlos Spencer was at first-five. So we never actually played a Colts test together.

By the end of 1994 Justin was having a groin problem and he was working with David Burk, the Canterbury team doctor. So there were a couple of connections there with Canterbury.

At the end of 1994 Graeme Bachop said he was going to Japan and Vance Stewart said to Justin, 'Look, we'll persist with you. We'll help with rehabilitation and so on'. I think it was the first real encouragement Justin had got for a while, and he made the decision to move from Southland.

Justin came to Canterbury for the 1995 season, with the encouragement of Vance, who knew what Justin could do.

He wasn't getting too much of a spin in Southland. They had another guy who was getting the run and I can remember watching Justin even having to play one game at fullback for a Colts team.

At the time I think he saw a bit of a wall in front of him in Southland. He went and had his operation, I think in Aussie, and after the operation I can remember Justin and I having a couple of rounds of golf together. There'd been a bit of that on the Colts tour, with Justin, Taine, Jeff and myself.

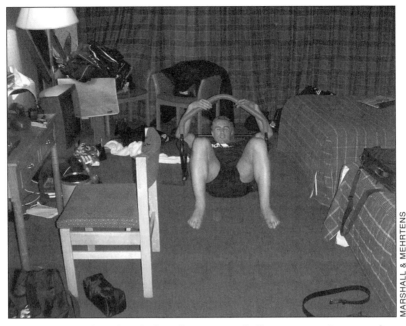

Working the abs. Justin has just enough floor space to exercise in his room during the '99 World Cup.

It was obvious during our rounds in 1995 that Justin was all fired up and doing his rehab so, come the start of the rugby season, he was into it.

He'd always been a sort of leader in terms of his actions in the team, but I think that from that point, perhaps because Canterbury had got in behind him so much, he became a lot more of a leader outside the actual on-the-field stuff.

We went really well until the end of the season in '95 and it was a great year for Justin. He'd started the year not even assured of a place in the Canterbury team, recovering from an injury. By the end of the year he was an All Black.

The All Black selectors had Stu Forster, Junior Tonu'u and Ant Strachan to go with, and suddenly Justin has leapt over all of them to be the No 1 halfback.

We started seeing a lot of each other in 1995 and at the end of the year we had the tour to Italy and France.

As a new kid, I'd been put on the laundry committee at the World Cup with Simon Culhane. I can say now with some considerable pride that I'd done such an outstanding job I was reappointed.

In fact, I was even more delighted when I discovered I'd been made Laundry Boss and my good friends Justin and Taine joined me on the Laundry Committee.

When we were in Auckland before we met, we went out and got these hats with 'Laundry' written on them. I had 'Laundry Boss' on mine. In fact, I've still got it. I think Justin's lost his, possibly out on the suds, but I think Taine will still have his unless, of course, he's eaten it.

Even though I got injured in Italy on that first part of the tour we had a card group of younger guys. We used to play a bit together, without wanting to be cliquey, because we were still youngsters.

Some of my memories from that time were the couple of times that Sean Fitzpatrick joined us. We played a game called Hole, in which there's a lot of abuse directed at the man who's the Hole.

So here's Fitzy, 10 years at the top, an absolute legend, and he comes and sits down with the youngest guys in the team and plays cards with us. **We were all a bit apprehensive at first, but then we started to have him on. He just laughed, took it, and fired it back.**

Two years later, when Fitzy was injured, Justin was given the All Black captaincy on the tour of England.

I thought it was absolutely the right decision. I know he doesn't like being the centre of attention off the field, although he deals with it well, but in terms of the on-the-field role, he's there at the coalface, he's fronting up, leading by example every game.

He's always demanding, but without making it sound like he's ordering, he's just wanting the best for the team. The guys really respond to that, the forwards especially.

Obviously the idea would have been past Fitzy, and he

would have seen exactly the same thing.

I think Justin's a natural captain, but I think he probably feels that his off-field profile wasn't seen as being ideal for what was wanted from an All Black captain at that time.

If you look at interviews with him back in 1997, he was reasonably tense, rather than his normal self. Thankfully, he's now back to his old self.

Another one I'd put in that category is Jonah. It's just nice to see guys now coming across on television as you know them, just answering and being natural.

What didn't help in 1997 was when Justin asked Jim Fleming something and he was marched 10. I don't think John Hart and some of the media liked the look of that, the captain getting marched for what was seen as dissent, which was very unfair. He did get slugged from behind by Martin Johnson, so he was pretty fired up.

It was disappointing to me to see how he was treated after that because at the end of the day the best thing we can do is our job on the field and, as far as I could see, he was the best man for the job.

I've always had huge respect for him because he can do everything. He's so gritty and gutsy. People see that.

He's also very fast, without looking as if he is. There are some guys who are just like that. Tabai Matson was one player who looked as if he was just gliding along when he was actually really moving.

Justin is quick. I know it's something that the boys are always chipping at each other over. He and Taine, when they do the tests over the first 10 metres, they're always giving it a nudge.

But in terms of straight out determination, when he puts his mind to it – and with a guy like Justin he doesn't cruise a lot – he is very quick.

One other thing I've found is, perhaps because we've played together so much, or because he's just naturally gifted, he can find me during a game with his passes.

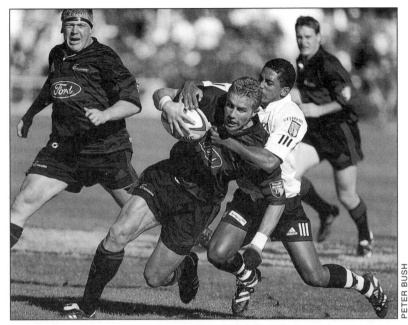

PETER BUSH

**Breyton Paulse puts the brakes on Justin during the Crusaders'
match with the Stormers in the 2000 Super 12.**

I'm often up in the air, changing and moving here and there, and even if he hasn't heard the call, he'll still find me, and react really quickly.

It's great to have a halfback who'll react so fast and will trust you as well. **Sometimes, if you've switched and the halfback goes to pass one way, then needs to swivel round, he'll hold back because he may be worried about an intercept coming from the blindside. Justin will still give it to me, because he trusts me to have called it right.**

As tough as he is, it has been hurtful that people suggest he doesn't clear the ball fast enough. In 1996 and 1997 nobody was saying things about Justin, but in 1998 nothing got going for us as a team. He seemed to cop a lot of the blame. It was very unfair.

Our ball was being slowed up horribly by an Aussie team which was very good at getting in on the ground and slowing it down, playing right to the edge of the laws.

At first-five I don't want to be shovelling on the ball when you've got big defensive lines coming up to knock the guys outside you down. So people were saying that we were kicking too much, and that a major reason for it was that the delivery from the halfback was slower than it had been.

The reality is that everything in rugby relies on everything else. But when people get on one tack it does become hurtful.

The best I can do about it with Justin is to be sensitive and caring. No, just kidding. Instead, I take the piss out of him every now and then.

I hassle him about tucking the ball under his arm and having a run. I say, 'I was so surprised for a start to actually get the ball, and then I was even more surprised when it was out in front of me, rather than above my head'. He'll say, 'Well, I'm surprised you didn't just kick it straight away.'

We do have our dust-ups. Not physical ones obviously. I'm not going to emerge too well from that.

We've had our moments at training. We were out at Burnham one year and I called something and he called something else. Anyway the ball got thrown out to me and I just thought, right, and kicked it straight down the field. I said, 'We want to do this, so we don't want the ball coming from there.'

He fired up and the next throw goes to the back of the lineout and the bullet I then got thrown at my head just about took it off!

In the end I find it frustrating because I find him a guy I can't really argue with. We argue on a different sort of level. I try to argue logically, but he just goes straight to the personal abuse.

When that happens we used to both just go silent. Early on that sort of silent thing would go on all day and we'd still be a little bit ginger around each other the next day.

But these days if we have a bit of a dust-up, the boys just stand around, have a bit of a chuckle under their breath while we're firing up at one another. But we'll sort it out quickly after training, which must be a sign that we're getting a bit of maturity creeping in.

We do see each other socially. You do often feel at certain times of the season, when it's been really busy, that ringing up a guy may be interfering with his personal time, with his wife or partner. But we see each other with our partners a lot for dinner and we golf a lot together, too.

There are things Justin does that most other people couldn't do. I respect that, and he knows that I do. He's unique.

We're very different people, but I do know that if there were people I really needed, then Justin and Nicole would be there.

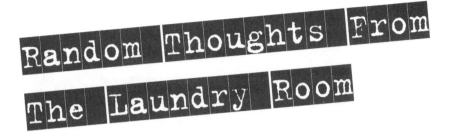

Random Thoughts From The Laundry Room

When you're the kings of the laundry room you often muse about what's been happening in the world outside soap suds and fabric softeners. Here are a few of those random moments.

IT CAN BE A TRIAL

In 1999 we played against New Zealand A, and that's always a shocker of a match. It was probably no better in the days when they had trials, but at least then people accepted that because it was trials, rugby mistakes would be made and the game would be messy.

In trials rugby the feeling was probably that it lacked shape because the combinations were reasonably new, but it was probably just as much because you know everyone so well, and are playing against guys you play with for weeks before it.

If you're in the All Blacks, playing New Zealand A you don't enjoy it because you're against guys you know well. **They're out to prove a point and the public generally backs the underdogs, so there's not too much support for you.**

THE EMBARRASSED CHEFS

Justin: At the start of the World Cup season the All Blacks stayed at the Fino Casementi apartments in Christchurch.

It was different from being in a normal hotel room, in that they were self contained units with kitchens. It was decided that the players would look after their own cooking and laundry, and be a bit more responsible for ourselves.

And one good thing we did do was have a cook-off. We were put into teams with the unit next to you, and we had a competition.

It actually developed a lot more than we thought it would. All of a sudden there were television cameras, photographers were taking pictures of guys in the kitchens, we were on the network news, and it all turned into a media event.

At the Big Fresh supermarket we were actually being trailed around by a TV crew. **That wasn't too good for Alama Ieremia and myself because we were on a budget that was supposed to be just for food. There were razor blades, shaving cream, underarm all going into the trolley.**

All sorts of things were being cooked up. Guys were doing entrees and desserts, people were making sushi, and marinating raw fish. I'd just thought that a few sizzlers would be nice.

Mehrts: It was intensely competitive. The guys were talking it up all day. We had a three course meal, starting with a carbonara. Anton Oliver followed up with a special fish and rice dish and Greg Feek chimed in with a magnificent banana dessert.

Justin: They had the hotel chef coming round with his big hat on, having a taste test and judging how we'd done. They were taking photos and making us pose beside our dishes.

That was very embarrassing for our team. We'd cooked a few sizzlers for an entree, then the traditional spaghetti bolognaise, and for dessert we had Mallow Puffs!

ATHLETIC SUPPORT

Justin: We played in the last test at Athletic Park before it was demolished. It's a ground I'd always liked. The atmosphere

PHOTOSPORT

Alas, Athletic Park, we knew her well. Mehrts and Justin loved the atmosphere at the famous old ground.

when the crowd packed in was fantastic, and whatever the weather might be, it was a hard place to beat. Wellington people do support the All Blacks. They get right in behind us.

You could feel the buzz around the town leading up to it and the drive to the park was a big thing. You could see all the people from the bus and you could feel the support.

Mehrts: The atmosphere at Athletic Park came from the people, not because it was designed to be purely a rugby ground. **Because it had such a low stand on one side, and such a high stand on the other, it actually felt more open than, say, Carisbrook.** It certainly didn't feel the way specific rugby grounds in South Africa do.

NO THREAT TO ELLE
Justin: When the All Blacks switched from the CCC jerseys, to adidas, five of us, Taine Randell, Anton Oliver, Mark

Hammett, Jeff Wilson and me, had to go to Auckland to show some of the new gear.

We had to come out first in training gear, then in track suits, and finally in the new jerseys. The final order was the rest of us, and then Taine, because he was the captain.

Just before we changed into jerseys I couldn't get my tracksuit pants off. The boys were waiting, yelling at me and eventually they took off on me! **So I was last out, shoe laces undone, looking untidy because I'd rushed so much, and I was pretty embarrasssed.**

Mehrts: It was a big job for adidas to take over after all the years that Canterbury had done the job. They did it pretty well.

As far as the design went, none of the players saw the jerseys before they were made public, but we were all happy with them.

Justin: We'd been expecting some sort of space age jerseys after all the publicity, but it maintained its tradition, which a lot of us like.

THE POLAR BLAST

Justin: I was rooming in Queenstown once with Taxi Maxwell in the All Blacks, and he hadn't seen a lot of snow.

He looked out the window of the hotel and said to me, 'I don't know whether we'll be able to do that training, eh?'

I said, 'Aw, what are you man? We'll be right. Look at that snow down there by the lake, it's almost all gone. We'll be right, don't worry about it, it'll be good as gold.'

Then, when the flippin' bus pulled up at training there was this massive big snow plough working away, and I could see Taxi glaring at me from the middle of the bus saying, 'What's the go here? You reckon there's no snow?'

The ground was covered in snow, and it was deep. We almost all started laughing, because we thought there was no way that we'd be training, but we went out anyway. They snow ploughed it and it turned to mud.

We could have flagged it, but the decision was made that we'd go out and in the end we trained really well. It was one

PHOTOSPORT

Dunedin's famous scarfies in full voice at Carisbrook during an Otago NPC match.

of those things that brings a team together. **You get tackled in a drill, skid over the ground on your back and a thin coating of ice goes inside your collar and down your back.**

You have a bit of a laugh while you're running through some thick snow to get to the field, but once you're out there it helps bond everyone.

SCARFIES
Dunedin's a good place to relax in. Even Jonah Lomu didn't get surrounded when we went to the movies there one night. It might be something to do with students. In Palmerston North it's much the same. They're not into looking like they care too much.

To be honest, in New Zealand there's no real problems for any player just wanting to cruise around town. Auckland's too big for anyone to worry too much, Wellington is so ethnically diverse it's easy, and in Christchurch people are generally very good. Really, the only place that rugby players get mobbed at all is South Africa.

DARE TO WIN

A big memory from Dunedin was the famous Richard Fry dare. Richard, who had played sevens for New Zealand in Hong Kong and was a good player for Counties, was All Black sponsorship manager for several years.

Mehrts: We were out at St Clair beach, just having a quiet meal. **Taine asked Richard what he would do if Taine stripped to his jocks, ran out into the water, stayed there for 90 seconds and ran back. It was freezing cold.**

Fryby said that he'd scull a jug and a half. So Taine did it, out in the water, back in. Fryby drank the beer. He wasn't that well and we noticed that he never agreed to a dare involving beer again.

It's a big thing, that dare stuff. We were at a camp in Palmerston North when Jonah said that he had spent two and a half minutes in a plunge pool that was chilled down to about 11 degrees.

Hatchet Oliver said that he could do three minutes, easily. So Taine said that if Hatchet could do that, we'd all drink two beers to every one that Hatchet drank. **And Hatchet did it, stepped out of the pool and drank two Steinies. Straight away we were all four down!**

THE RULES

We often go out in our mini-teams that we have inside the All Blacks, and we like to set ourselves a standard straight away by having a big dinner, all of us hitting McDonald's.

There was a rule once in Tauranga that you had to double up. Once we'd finished at McDonald's you had to eat something at KFC. If you didn't you'd be ostracised by the group and you'd have to walk home as well. We were staying at Mt Maunganui and from Tauranga to the Mount is a fair stretch.

Wherever the All Blacks might be, there's never a McDonald's too far away.

THE NIGHT TIME MAY OR MAY NOT BE THE RIGHT TIME

The first night test in Auckland was against Australia two years ago, and night games still get a mixed reaction.

Mehrts: A lot of guys don't like them because they're used to their routine during the day, and getting the game over with. Toddy Blackadder really doesn't like them.

Justin: I don't like them.

Mehrts: I enjoy them. I really like sitting round, having a wee snooze during the day and having enough time to feel organised. **To be fair, I don't think the players who don't like night games have a problem with them, just that a lot would prefer the day games.**

When there's a night game, management like us to just crash out and read a book, or go to sleep, to get away from it. They encourage us to not watch rugby if there's an afternoon game on television. You can get too hyped up.

Before a night game everything is the same as an afternoon game. We have lunch up until about 4pm, which is the same as an 11am lunch for an afternoon game. The backs and forwards, just to break up the day, will get together at about 11 o'clock. The forwards will go through lineouts, the backs will talk through what moves we might try.

SNORING ALL THE WAY TO JO'BURG

When we do South African flights, the management try to get us into our South African sleep patterns as quickly as possible. **We usually arrive in South Africa early in the morning, so they're happy for us to sleep on the leg from Perth to Johannesburg.**

But they do want us to stay awake between Sydney and Perth, which means that we're looking to keep awake from midnight to 6am New Zealand time.

Then the guys that want, get a sleeping pill from Doc Mayhew and sleep all the way to South Africa, where we then try to stay awake all the first day, which is not the easiest thing to do.

There's no hassle if you don't want to take sleeping pills, but they encourage you to do so, and they also give you a two litre bottle of water that they expect you to drink between Sydney and Perth, and then another one they want drunk between Perth and Jo'burg.

Justin: Mehrts really battles with the water.

Mehrts: I never drink water. I wouldn't drink two litres of water in a week!

Justin: If it was Coke he'd be alright. He'd get through two litres of that, no problem.

Mehrts: I do drink orange juice, and some soft drinks. I just don't drink a lot of water.

As it happens, I don't like sleeping on a plane either, so I try to watch movies, or play with a computer. I find it works well for me, because when we get there, and I stay awake the first day, by the time night comes I'm totally wasted and I get to

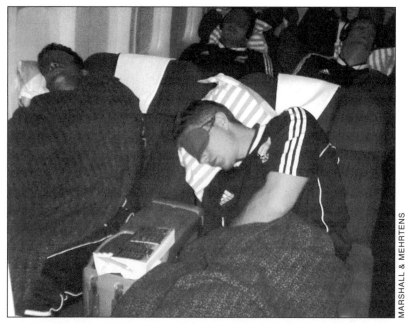

MARSHALL & MEHRTENS

Justin is out for the count during another long-haul flight with the All Blacks.

sleep without having to bother about sleeping pills.

Justin: A couple of times I've caught you drifting off, though.

Mehrts: I sure do. But for what it's worth, my tip is to waste yourself.

Justin: What I do is, that night, when you've stayed awake for the whole day over there, you have a couple of beers before you go to bed, and you go to sleep right away.

Mehrts: Of course, all the management tell you to stay awake, Sydney to Perth, and if you walk down the aisle there's all of them, all toast, sound asleep.

DARE TO WIN II

Sun City, the famous resort in South Africa, is a very relaxing place, entirely safe, except for the hippos. There's a wildlife resort out the back of Sun City that has a really fantastic range of animals. The big tip is to make sure you don't stand between the hippos and the water.

On one visit, when Ravishing Richard Fry was with the team, there was a news story from Thailand about a dwarf who had been eaten by a hippo.

So someone said, 'Right, well if Richard Fry stands in front of the water for 30 minutes, let's see if he can run faster than 40km/h, because that's how fast they say a hippo can run.'

There were a number of guys who were quite prepared to face the jug and a half penalty if it meant Richard would take the dare on. He didn't.

HIGH AND DRY

The first time you actually train at altitude in South Africa is tough. The third day there is normally the hardest.

That's supposed to be the time when your body has depleted its stores of haemoglobin, and it then starts to build up again until it's back to normal after seven days.

It's the third day there that we usually have our first tough training session. **It's dry, it's hot and you get tired very fast. You get a dry nose, dry throat and your legs start getting rubbery. You just get exhaused a lot more quickly.**

They're fanatical about their rugby in South Africa. The All Blacks went to one training run in Pretoria and just a couple of metres off the end of the training field there were a group of local guys who had fired up a huge big barbecue. So as you were training there was smoke and cooking smells wafting over the ground.

When you come down to breakfast at the hotel you can guarantee that there will be a group of people waiting in the foyer wanting to get autographs.

Pretoria's actually not a bad place to be because there are not so many things to do that you want to get out of the hotel that much.

There's a movie theatre just across the next intersection, no more than two minutes walk away. So even if you go to the movies at night, it's safe to be on the street in a small group.

One thing we did do on one trip was go to Pretoria Zoo, which was fascinating. They've got everything there, from gorillas, to bears, to a little lion cub and a big enclosure for the elephants that's surrounded by a moat, so the feeling is very free and open. The giraffes could walk across the fence if they wanted to. It was really good fun.

Super Three-peat

The record of the Crusaders in Super 12 is remarkable. In the first year of the competition, 1996, the Crusaders were dead last. In the famous words of Todd Blackadder: 'When we came back into the changing room, we were looking for ropes slung over the beams'. The next year, with Wayne Smith at the coaching helm, they advanced to sixth and then, in 1998, as rank outsiders, they beat the Blues in a pulsating final at Eden Park. In 1999 they went to the House of Pain, Carisbrook, where they scored a convincing victory over the Highlanders. At the start of the 2000 season they stood poised to become the first team to win Super 12 three times in a row.

When the Crusaders first got together in 2000 it was mentioned that we had the chance to make some Super 12 history – the three-peat and all that – but we really tried to play it down, because it wasn't an issue.

When we sorted out the team values for the season we had the same team values that we'd had for the previous two seasons. **Everybody starts Super 12 wanting to win it, but we wanted to take that whole concept out of it. We just wanted to win it for its own sake.**

That probably shone through when we won it because we

weren't thinking, 'Yeah, third time we've won it'. We were just happy to win it and to have beaten a good team made it worthwhile.

We took it right out and didn't want to make an issue of it, not make it part of our everyday vision. So it didn't come into the team culture at all.

We were in Westport for five days and had one day in Greymouth. It was stinking hot in Westport for the week, which was tough on guys who were mingling with the local people.

There are promotional things we do. We play in Timaru, but the last couple of years we haven't played on the Coast. So we spend time there and when you're doing promotional work for DB, it's probably better to do it early in the season rather than in the middle.

We'd start off with an early session, maybe seven to eight. When you do first get into it, you get very sore. Then we'd have training at 10. Pretty full on and really sweating it out. **After lunch we'd let the food digest, have a meeting, go over the team culture and get committees formed for the year – the organisation. Then train again and maybe do a promotion.**

It's all part of it and most of the jokers find it pretty enjoyable.

There never seems to be any problems fitting in the guys from outside of Canterbury. They seem to just slip in without a hitch.

Part of it is the guys that they choose, not just for their ability, but the all-round thing. Norm Berryman came in and from the first meeting he was a laugh a minute.

The only criteria is that you have to be able to laugh at yourself because we do take the piss out of everyone. Just to be able to laugh at yourself really evens things out.

Robbie Deans is just like a senior player. While he's the coach, he's not that long out of the playing ranks. It's a bit like having a really senior, senior player involved in the team. Somebody who is able to take control of the team and to also have that wealth of experience on his side.

He does present a fairly serious sort of exterior to the public, but he balances that up with the team. We can chip him at training and have a laugh, yet still not lose respect for him.

He's very competitive and he took on a whole new role in 2000. He had previously been the manager, but he was so intent on the team doing well and doing his job with the team that he never, ever encroached on the coaching of Smithy or Sloaney.

If they wanted to go to him and discuss something, they would have been able to go to him, and it must have happened. But the players never saw him in any role other than that of the manager.

As coach, he did try to be the manager for a while. He just wants the best, because you know that his heart's in it.

Justin: He's a fantastic coach, who has gained a lot of respect because of his achievements, especially as a Canterbury player. When you look at Robbie Deans, you don't so much look at him as an All Black player – and he was a great All Black – but more of what he did for Canterbury.

The guys in this area really know that we've got a bit of a legend here. But we never tell him that.

We played *Give It A Boot Robbie* **at a session once, just so he knew that while we do consider him something of a legend, we'll still take the piss out of him.**

There's that side of him, but there's also the side that shows up in his coaching. He's been through all the courses in Wellington and he has a very, very good mind for the game.

Mehrts: He's a meticulous planner, something that's very similar to Smithy. He loves things being simple and likes asking questions of the guys. Why did they do this? Why did you do that?

He's also quite happy to trust the players within that. He just knows the game.

Justin: He always challenges us at training. He's prepared to try something new, that's game related, but if the drill doesn't work, he's not the sort of person whose ego is so big he says, 'Bugger you, you'll work on it until you've got it right'. We'll tell him if it doesn't work.

Mehrts: We'll tell him for days!

Both: He's got his favourite sayings. 'You have to change the picture all the time' and 'keep it simple.'

When he was the manager he was involved in the team, but he made the change from being the manager to coach really well. It could have got stale, but it didn't. When he went to coach it was a brand new set of ideas.

A lot of the basics are the same as with Smithy, but there are differences. Robbie will coach the way he wants to coach.

Robbie will decide what direction the team's going to be going in and then he coaches the skills that are needed for that. For example, in Westport this year everyone realised that there was likely to be a bit more attacking kicking with the big defensive lines.

So it wasn't as if Robbie sent the forwards away to do lineouts, while the backs worked on grubber kicks. We had everyone working on kicks and their skills. So that was good for the team and good for the direction we were all going in.

Game one: February 27

The Crusaders beat the Chiefs 27–24 in Hamilton. A dropped goal by Aaron Mauger put the Crusaders in the lead four minutes from the end and then the Chiefs' Glen Jackson missed a 30-metre penalty goal that would have given the Chiefs the draw.

For the Crusaders: Tries by Todd Blackadder and Caleb Ralph; four penalty goals and a conversion by Andrew Mehrtens; dropped goal by Aaron Mauger.

For the Chiefs: Tries by Loki Crichton and Chresten Davis; four penalty goals and a conversion by Glen Jackson.

The year could have started very badly again against the Chiefs. Every year we always talk about how we have to get away to a good start and get a couple of wins under our belts.

We'd bet that every team says the same thing.

Mehrts: It's a question of not only getting away to a solid enough start, but leaving room to keep improving. **We do want week to week improvement and we've based a lot of our play on that in the last three years, developing things as we go through.**

If you look at developing your own play, it makes it easier to adapt when you come up against different sorts of teams. It makes it easier to change your own plan, based on who you're playing.

Whereas, if you start off with a hiss and a roar and fire all your shots, it makes it very difficult to change that. That's why teams like the Waratahs struggle. They have a massive pre-season and always give everyone a hiding before the competition starts. Then they launch into Super 12 and just self-destruct.

We always plays Waikato and Auckland quite early and we always have the bye early.

Game two: March 10

The Crusaders beat the Blues 32–20 in Christchurch. Coming off a bye, the Crusaders scored their first ever win over the Blues in Christchurch. They raced to an 18–10 lead in the first half, but the Blues rallied, without ever getting closer than six points adrift.

For the Crusaders: Tries by Scott Robertson, Leon MacDonald and Caleb Ralph; three penalty goals, two dropped goals and a conversion by Andrew Mehrtens.

For the Blues: Tries by Troy Flavell (2) and Mark Robinson; penalty goal and a conversion by Hayden Taylor.

Game three: March 18

The Crusaders beat the Queensland Reds 27–19 in Brisbane. The game that marked Todd Blackadder becoming the first New Zealander to play 50 Super 12 games looked like being a horror show for the Crusaders. At halftime they trailed 16–3, but 10 minutes into the second half came an 80-metre intercept try from Justin Marshall that turned the game.

For the Crusaders: Tries by Justin Marshall, Leon MacDonald and Ron Cribb; two penalty goals and three conversions by Andrew Mehrtens.
For the Reds: Try by Chris Latham; four penalty goals and a conversion by Shane Drahm.

Both: We won a bit more often early in 2000, but we still didn't really get it together until we were under some pressure against Queensland. It wasn't quite as hot in 2000 as it had been in previous years, but it was still sweaty.

Pre-season a couple of years ago we played there and some of the forwards at halftime just went and lay down in cold showers, let the water run on them for 10 minutes.

Mehrts: We were down before Justin got his runaway try. That was a massive try. It was essentially a 14-point try; they were hot on attack and likely to score.

Justin: Does there feel like a lot of space in front of you when you get an intercept inside your 22? It actually feels more like there's an awful lot of speed out there to catch you.

That's one of the few intercept tries I've ever scored. The best thing about it was that they were wanting to move it back inside to Chris Latham. So that takes the fullback out of the equation.

But for somebody like me, who hasn't got the fastest set of legs in the team, knowing that you probably haven't got a lot of support is not a nice feeling.

Mehrts: You knew that I'd be 40 metres back cheering you on. Standing on halfway clapping, calling, 'Go son!'

Justin: It just came at an opportune time, because it kicked us into gear a little bit. We weren't playing well and were sort of mediocre, but then we got desperate and we took off.

Game four: March 26

The Crusaders beat the Stormers 47–31 in Nelson. In brilliant sunshine, in front of a capacity crowd of 15,000, there were 10 tries scored, and No 8 Ron Cribb was so sensational he was suddenly an All Black prospect.

For the Crusaders: Tries by Marika Vunibaka (2), Justin Marshall, Todd Blackadder, Caleb Ralph and Ron Cribb; three penalty goals and four conversions by Andrew Mehrtens.

For the Stormers: Tries by Chean Roux (2), Cobus Visagie and De Wet Barry; penalty goal and two conversions by Braam van Stratten; conversion by Percy Montgomery; conversion by Dan van Zyl.

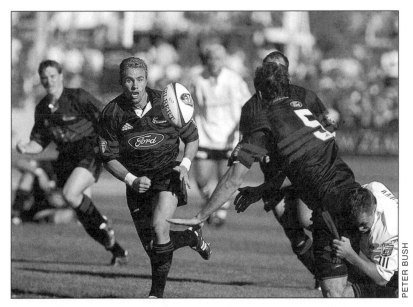

PETER BUSH

Norm Maxwell feeds Justin during the high-scoring 2000 Super 12 match against the Stormers in Nelson.

Both: Generally we were a lot more consistent this year in the round robin, but the nature of the competition is that if you don't play well, the odds are you'll lose.

There were some great moments. In Nelson against the Stormers we had a high-scoring game on a beautiful day – Ron Cribb buried Percy Montgomery in a massive tackle in that game. We hear Percy's still there. They've erected a headstone for him.

We had Marika Vunibaka from the Fijian team last year. He's so very fast that we reckon we only saw him fully open out once. You can tell when he's really flat out because he gets what looks like a big grin on his face, baring his teeth.

Once he did it in a game and the other time was at a speed training drill. We were in a front group, which had run 60 metres, and he was in the second group. We turned to watch him and someone must have chipped him or something. He absolutely let loose for the last 20 or 30 metres. **He's frighteningly fast that joker and, like Robbie says, he's very smart, although he's quite shy.**

He and Afato So'oalo spend a fair bit of time together. They've both had to adjust to an entirely different culture and climate.

Game five: April 1

The Crusaders beat the Highlanders 40–36 in Christchurch. The game of two halves has rarely been as starkly demonstrated. The Crusaders led 32–12 at halftime, but the last 30 minutes belonged largely to the Highlanders, who scored one try from a movement that began when Marc Ellis ran from behind his own goal-line.

For the Crusaders: Tries by Ron Cribb (2), Norm Berryman, Marika Vunibaka and Caleb Ralph; three penalty goals and three conversions by Andrew Mehrtens.

For the Highlanders: Tries by Karl Te Nana, Kelvin Middleton, Rua Tipoki and Pita Alatini; three penalty goals, conversion and a dropped goal by Tony Brown; conversion by Tipoki.

Game six: April 7

The Hurricanes beat the Crusaders 28–22 in Wellington. Down in the first minute, when Jonah Lomu scored a try, the Crusaders fought back to be 14–all at halftime. But Christian Cullen and Lomu got the Hurricanes back in front and, despite being hard on attack for the last 10 minutes, the game slipped away from the Crusaders.

For the Crusaders: Tries by Marika Vunibaka and Todd Blackadder; four penalty goals by Andrew Mehrtens.

For the Hurricanes: Tries by Jonah Lomu (2) and Christian Cullen (2); four conversions by David Holwell.

PETER BUSH

Reuben Thorne prepares to engage the Hurricanes during the Crusaders' sixth round loss in Wellington.

Game seven: April 15

The Crusaders beat the Sharks 32–24 in Durban. The Sharks ran it at the Crusaders and although there were errors, the Crusaders were usually in control. After slipping to third on the points table with their loss to the Hurricanes, the Crusaders were back on top at the end of the weekend, the Brumbies being upset by the Waratahs.

For the Crusaders: Tries by Caleb Ralph, Leon MacDonald, Mark Mayerhofler and Ron Cribb; two penalty goals and three conversions by Andrew Mehrtens.

For the Sharks: Tries by Pieter Muller (2), and Jacques Greeff; penalty goal and three conversions by Gaffie du Toit.

145

When we went to South Africa we played the Sharks and the Cats. The Sharks didn't have a good year, but it was still nice to beat them in Durban.

Game eight: April 22

The Cats beat the Crusaders 54–31 in Johannesburg. Todd Blackadder didn't mince words. 'We were outplayed and had to try catch-up rugby for much of the game'.

For the Crusaders: Tries by Greg Feek, Afato So'oalo and Leon MacDonald; four penalty goals and two conversions by Andrew Mehrtens:

For the Cats: Tries by Thinus Delport (2), Werner Swanepoel, Grant Esterhuizen, Japie Mulder and Johan Erasmus; three penalty goals, six conversions and a dropped goal by Louis Koen.

When we played the Cats we were down by heaps, and came back, but they skipped away again. It wasn't anything to do with fitness, it was just one of those games.

Sometimes you get to a position where you're just a point behind and you get a roll on. But against the Cats that didn't happen.

Game nine: April 28

The Crusaders beat the Bulls 75–27 in Christchurch. A sparkling effort by the Crusaders, which yielded 11 tries, but a rib injury to Andrew Mehrtens that would keep him out of the next week's game against the Waratahs.

For the Crusaders: Tries by Caleb Ralph (3), Marika Vunibaka (3), Justin Marshall (2), Scott Robertson, Chris Jack and Dallas Seymour; conversions by Andrew Mehrtens (4) and Aaron Mauger (6).

For the Bulls: Tries by Jaco van der Westhuyzen, Henry Pedro and Frikkie Welsh; penalty goal, three conversions and a dropped goal by Jannie de Beer.

Game ten: May 5

The Crusaders beat the Waratahs 22–13 in Christchurch. A tough, bruising battle which, in the words of coach Robbie Deans, saw the Crusaders 'guts it out'. The win was followed by a Brumbies victory over the Reds, which made the Brumbies top of the table again, and the next weekend's Crusaders–Brumbies clash at Jade Stadium the game to probably decide where the 2000 final would be played.

For the Crusaders: Tries by Marika Vunibaka (2), Leon MacDonald and Justin Marshall; conversion by MacDonald.

For the Waratahs: Try by Christian Warner; two penalty goals and a conversion by Matt Burke.

Game eleven: May 12

The Brumbies beat the Crusaders 17–12 in Christchurch. How well the Brumbies maintained possession can be judged by the fact that in the first half, the Crusaders had one throw to the lineout, while the Brumbies had 13. How well the Crusaders defended can be measured by the fact the Brumbies only scored two tries.

For the Crusaders: Four penalty goals by Leon MacDonald.

For the Brumbies: Tries by Andrew Walker and Mitch Hardy; penalty goal and two conversions by Stirling Mortlock.

We were at home to the Brumbies at Jade Stadium and they're a daunting team to play against. They're always asking questions of the defence.

They do the thing you can do best against the defensive systems now, and that's hold the ball. Eventually the defence is going to crack.

They're very good at that, to the extent that they sometimes don't commit themselves to tackles. If they think they're going to get smashed, they'll simply go to ground and recycle the ball.

It's difficult to play without the ball for long periods. In that first game they had something like 70 per cent of the possession. It becomes draining. They get the ball and you think, 'God, we're going to have to hold on for another 15 phases.'

It's easy for a referee to start looking at the offside line when you're playing against the Brumbies. The odds are, just thinking logically, that if you're getting up to so many phases, that someone is going to be offside.

You've got to be thinking, 'Well, someone is going to be getting eager'. A lot of it depends on the timing, and because they clean the ball out so well, and so quickly, every now and then someone in the defence is going to think it's out and have a go.

The frustrating thing is that if you give it away easily when you get the ball, as we did at times that night, it makes it very difficult. **We shut them down pretty well and they only scored two tries, despite all the ball they had.**

Justin: It is difficult with their dummy runners, too. I remember in that game at Jade Stadium they were, at times, bloody annoying. Off the lineout you'd find players in front of you and they'd run the ball behind players – they have that down to a sort of an art.

There was one game they played, against the Waratahs, where Paddy O'Brien picked them up a lot. They lost that game.

Mehrts: I think we've always been a pretty fair team. If you look at our guys at the back of a ruck, like Scott Robertson, if he's out of the play he'll flatten himself down so as to not interfere with the play.

They have faith in the amount of hard work they've done to get to where they want to be, so we'll usually allow a foot behind the line to avoid being penalised.

Semifinal: May 20

The Crusaders beat the Highlanders 37–15 in Christchurch. Justin Marshall and Norm Maxwell were both out of the semifinal when they were injured at the final training run. A 21-year-old, Ben Hurst, played his first Super 12 game. He was behind a pack who would dominate play.

For the Crusaders: Tries by Marika Vunibaka (2) and Ron Cribb; six penalty goals and two conversions by Andrew Mehrtens.

For the Highlanders: Tries by Simon Maling and Byron Kelleher; penalty goal by Tony Brown; conversion by Brendon Laney.

PETER BUSH

Marika Vunibaka – when the big grin begins, the after-burners kick in.

Justin: I came out of the Brumbies game with a judicial meeting to go to before the semifinal against the Highlanders.

They were going to ban me for a week if I didn't make an apology. So I did what they wanted, then went to training and tore a calf muscle.

What happened in the game was that we had a maul under control about five metres from the line and the referee, Andre Watson, told me to clear the ball. I said, 'It's still moving'. He said, 'Clear it'. So then I started yelling for the ball and he blew it. I said, 'Aw ---- Andre.'

Then I saw him reach for the card in his pocket. So I said, 'I'll save you the bloody trouble', and I started walking off.

The next day he said he was reaching in his pocket for the yellow card. But in all the confusion – me walking off and Toddy going to him, 'What the hell's going on?' – when I came back he said he was going to penalise me.

Mehrts: Justin was struck down by the Black Widow, Daryl Gibson. Any time there's an injury in the Crusaders, there'll be a Gibson connection there somewhere.

He threw the pass when Justin blew his Achilles out in 1998. He was the one who knocked on when there was a scrum on the line and Matt Sexton blew out his Achilles. He passed the ball to Norm Maxwell once when Maxi was hurt, and he was actually passing the ball to Justin at Rugby Park when Justin tore his calf muscle. You stay away from Gibbo at training!

Justin: In the semifinal we struck Otago. It was a pretty convincing win in my memory.

In the final in Canberra I could probably have played, but I would have only been at about 50 per cent.

Mehrts: So, better than usual?

Justin: I guess so, but it wouldn't have been the right thing by the team.

Mehrts: It's actually tough for the rest of us watching a player like Justin, who has done everything to get the injury right and so obviously wants to play, but can't get out there.

Justin: That's a large part of what you play your season for. **You go through the round-robin to hopefully get to the semifinal and then you win that and blow it at training. It's bloody hard.**

Mehrts: It happened to me in South Africa in 1996 and no matter what anybody says about what you've done to get the side there, you still don't feel part of the team somehow.

I played in the Tri-Nations game, in Cape Town, that wasn't considered part of the test series. Then I was out with a training injury for the two tests that we won, then played in the one at Ellis Park that we lost.

So I still struggle to feel that I was fully part of that series win in South Africa.

Final: May 27

The Crusaders beat the Brumbies 20–19 in Canberra. This really was an epic encounter, with the odds stacked against the Crusaders. In fact, the TAB were offering $2.40 for a Crusaders win and just $1.50 for the Brumbies.

For the Crusaders: Try by Ron Cribb; five penalty goals by Andrew Mehrtens.

For the Brumbies: Try by George Smith; four penalty goals and a conversion by Stirling Mortlock.

Justin: I was sitting down at the edge of the ground with the boys for the final, and it was really cold. It had been snowing during the day and they predicted it to get even worse!

Canberra's not the warmest place in Australia at the best of times, so it wasn't a pleasant day.

Mehrts: The wind wasn't as bad as people made it out to be and once you're running around it's not too bad. I didn't wear thermals because I get too hot, but I guess the guys out on the wings had to.

We all knew that we hadn't played that well against the Brumbies at Jade Stadium and while they are very good, they are a bit one-dimensional.

It can be easier sometimes to get motivated in a game that's away from home. Even during the day before, when you're just relaxing and enjoying yourself, you've got that game in the back of your mind and it's easier to remember what you're there for.

At home you're seeing friends, doing other things and it can distract you just a little bit.

For a team with a culture like ours, it's not the daunting prospect that you might expect.

It was also good this time, the feeling that we were playing for the country, not just for the Crusaders.

On the day before the final the kickers went down to the ground for a session a wee bit earlier than the rest of the team.

But on the Friday in Canberra it was so cold that all we did was run round and play a bit of force 'em back. I hadn't had any kicks at goal at all and when the team turned up I thought, 'Gee, the coaches are here, I'd better take some kicks.'

So I knocked over five in a row from quite wide out on the right hand side, then went out to the other side, knocked over five from there and thought, 'Bugger this, my rhythm's good, leave it'. There's no point in kicking them until your leg comes off. Funnily enough, with the boys there and a bit of pressure on, I was striking them well.

Early on I swapped back to fullback quite a lot. Just seeing our defensive line moving up, getting forward, almost like sumo wrestlers and knocking them over, I had a huge amount of confidence. In the first half they had to resort a few times to kicking and putting up up-and-unders, which was encouraging.

I just thought, 'The guys have got the adrenalin and confidence to keep this going for the whole 80 minutes'. Even though there was only one point in it at the end, it felt good for the whole game.

Ron Cribb's a great guy who's fitted in really well and he's done the hard work, so it was nice to see him getting the try for all his efforts with his little 'nudge' through.

Then in the final few minutes there was a penalty to get us ahead. I'd been getting cramp in both legs at the time. It's not so bad running around, it's when you tense up and extend your legs, as if you're going up on tip-toes. So making a tackle seems to bring it on.

Towards the end I can remember making a tackle and then just sort of sitting beside the ruck, sticking my legs straight out in front of me like a little kid at school. The cramp was probably a mixture of the cold and having had a stiff back for a couple of weeks before. My back was terrible during the semifinal against the Highlanders, but it was a lot better in Canberra.

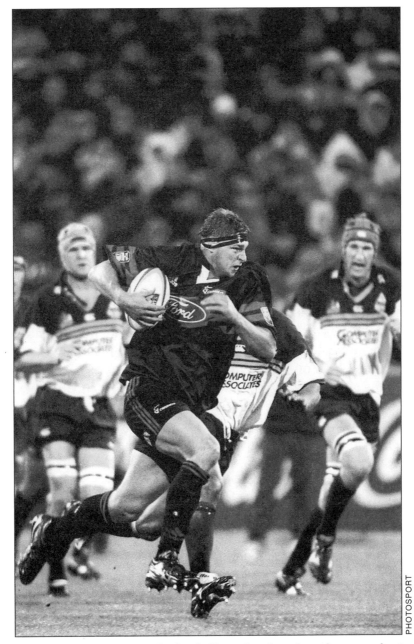

PHOTOSPORT

When Toddy's hot, he's hot! Here he breaks clear against Brumbies in the Super 12 final.

Even kicking to touch when you're just tensing your leg, that's when it really grips. You can actually do any sort of kicking, but then, on your follow through, it really grips hold of you.

At that last kick I was worried I'd be in some sort of pain after the kick, and that it might make me hold back. So I tried really hard to just give it everything, just whack it . . . and then it's over and whatever happens won't matter if you've kicked the ball properly. It did come off nicely and in the end I don't think I even cramped up.

Justin: After the game we had a big team session. The team room was on the ground floor of the hotel, not far from where the main lobby bar was.

Most of the people who were over there from Canterbury were staying at the same hotel as us. Once we'd had the team session we just opened the doors and people came in.

Mehrts: It was a really big team room. When we first came in, people were in the lobby and they gave us a cheer, then we went and got changed and had our wee session.

It didn't go on for too long. At the end of our session a few of the guys knew people who were outside. They invited them in for a drink – along with heaps of other people – and by the end of it we just had a whole conference room full of red and black. It was great.

At times I just sort of hung on the fringe and watched the celebrations, which was a good feeling.

My old man was there, which was also great. He stayed up until about four o'clock, which was pretty late for him. I was happy about the whole thing.

Justin: Scott Robertson and I did go and see the Brumbies. I'd been talking to George Gregan after the game and asked where he was going.

We went to the bar that the Brumbies must go to all the time. It wasn't too crowded, so it turned out to be a good night.

Stirling Mortlock said to me that night, 'Yeah, it was a bit of a bugger. If I'd kicked a few more it might have been a better

PHOTOSPORT

It's a third straight Super 12 title and the boys are all feeling pretty pleased with themselves.

night'. Guys like Jim Williams and Rod Kafer – a lot of them, really – are good blokes. While they were disappointed, they were welcoming.

Mehrts: You can identify with their disappointment easily enough. They'd done a lot of hard work, they'd played as a team; the things that'd we'd like to pride ourselves on. Rod McQueen is a good bloke, too.

After the game we had a massive few days. The next morning we had to be up early to fly through Sydney airport to get home and, not surprisingly, we were all pretty seedy. We weren't good sights.

Then we had a couple of days of celebrations and the culmination was the parade, where we had good weather again. Then it was back to the Cotswold Hotel. We had a team photo and then we all went to the Lancaster Hotel.

We had a few drinks and a few racing games where you drop

a peanut into your beer and see whose stays down the longest. Justin must have won about six in a row and he named his peanut 'Sub Merge'.

He started racing Sub Merge off against other peanuts and he was so good that Marshy eventually put him in his shirt pocket. The next morning he found him on the bedroom floor.

Then we all said, 'Wouldn't it be nice if we all went and had a beer in the middle of Lancaster Park'. It's a tradition that Otago have, where they all go at the end of the season and have a drink in the middle of Carisbrook.

We started organising kegs, so by the time we got to the park there were shadows all over the ground. So we all went and sat up on the embankment, which we knew was going to go at some point in the future.

We all hung out up there at the back of the embankment for a couple of hours, just all the boys. It was a really nice time, all the boys on the bank.

It's always a bit sad when the campaign comes to an end. You've all trained hard through the summer and pretty much every team and every player is at their peak. It was a great time and a great bunch of jokers to be involved with.

Tri As We Might

The All Blacks went into Tri-Nations 2000 after three warm-up games, a 102–0 demolition of Tonga and two convincing victories over Scotland, 48-14, and 69–20. But they knew the real measure of the season would be in the toughest international competition in the world.

Tri-Nations I: July 15

The All Blacks beat Australia 39–35 at Stadium Australia, Sydney.
For the All Blacks: Tries by Tana Umaga, Pita Alatini, Christian Cullen, Justin Marshall and Jonah Lomu; two penalty goals and four conversions by Andrew Mehrtens.
For Australia: Tries by Stirling Mortlock (2), Chris Latham, Joe Roff and Jeremy Paul; two penalty goals and two conversions by Mortlock.

Both: In the first 20 or 30 minutes, whoever had the ball dominated completely.

Justin: After 10 minutes Australia hadn't touched the ball, except to kick off, and we were 21 points in front. It was going so well, we just wanted to retain the ball.

Then we finally lost a kickoff, they regained it, there wasn't a stoppage and they scored. Then they scored, and scored again. It was a weird sort of feeling.

Mehrts: It was one of those games where you get that rare, exhilarating feeling where everything goes well, and after 15 minutes you're pinching yourself to make sure it's true.

It seldom happens. Once was in the 1995 World Cup semifinal against England in South Africa, when we kicked away to a big win.

In Sydney I was thinking that everything we'd practised was coming off. Obviously the Aussies then regrouped and thought about it, and worked their game out better and started coming back.

Justin: Once they got it, they did some very good things with the ball. So at halftime, at 24-all, it was basically back to the drawing board.

Mehrts: We went into the game fizzing. We'd seen the Wallabies win the World Cup in 1999 and we were at a stage of the season where everyone in the team was at a peak.

There had been enough hard rugby in Super 12 to get us right, the scenery was still very fresh in the All Blacks, and with the three games we'd had leading into the Tri-Nations, combinations had the chance to develop.

I'd say we were at an equivalent point to where the French were when we played them in November. The game in Sydney, especially the start, was probably the peak of our season.

Contrary to what may be a popular belief, rugby players don't get into a lead and then sit back thinking, 'We can all go home now, we've won the game'. In fact, if anything the last few years has taught us in the All Blacks, it's that no matter what the lead is, the other team can come back. Other teams have done it to us and we've done it several times ourselves.

So when we get a good lead, there's an absolute determination from everyone not to stuff up. **On this occasion we certainly didn't ease off. The fact was that Australia got hold of the ball and they used it very effectively.**

When the Aussies came back we knew that it was because they were holding possession, and so it was essential for us to do the same. The start had certainly helped our confidence there, because we knew that they weren't unbeatable.

Justin's try in the second half came from a kickoff. Ron

A world record crowd of 110,000 people at Stadium Australia for the Tri-Nations opener at Sydney.

Cribb popped the ball up to him and he ran a hell of a long way, stepping and shrugging guys off for the try.

Justin: Mehrts reckons that he put the ball exactly on the 10 metre line so we could win it back, but then he would say that, wouldn't he?

It was off a kickoff. Cribby picked it up and I was lucky enough to be on the outside of him.

Mehrts: At that point it was a really good try for Justin to score. It wasn't necessarily a big moment in terms of how his game had been going, but people saw it and started saying, 'This is the Justin of old.'

He'd had a lot of criticism during the year, which from my perspective is hard, especially when a guy who you play alongside on the field, who's a bloody good mate, is copping flak. It's even harder when you don't believe it was justified, which I never have.

We actually deal with that by chipping each other. I never hesitate to point out people who say he's got a slow pass, which he doesn't, and he comes back at me with the 'kicks too much' comment.

Justin: When I came off late in the game we were in the lead, but then Jeremy Paul got a try in the corner and they seemed to be on a roll. But then we got that fabulous try to Jonah. It was then we had the win.

Tri-Nations II: July 22

The All Blacks beat South Africa 25–12 at Jade Stadium, Christchurch.

For the All Blacks: Two tries by Christian Cullen; three penalty goals and a dropped goal by Andrew Mehrtens; dropped goal by Tony Brown.

For South Africa: Three penalty goals by Braam van Straaten; dropped goal by Percy Montgomery.

Both: We were always expected to win this game after our win at Stadium Australia, but it was tougher than it may have looked.

Justin: It wasn't the free-flowing spectacle that we'd had the week before. We went from a game in Sydney that had the whole country buzzing to a match that was dominated by some pretty rugged defence.

It was an old-fashioned, hard-nosed test without the thrills of the week before, but lots of hard yakker.

Mehrts: It was a pretty ugly sort of game. It was dour, but we fronted and the South Africans are always very tough physically; they're always passionate and committed.

Justin: The South Africans are big boys and they usually like to gain some physical dominance before they start throwing the ball around and using backs like Breyton Paulse.

By comparison, the Australians may not look to dominate physically, but are happier to use their skills at any stage in the game.

Against South Africa you know you're in for a match where they'll try to smash you around and if you don't give as good as you take, you'll end up in a world of hurt.

Mehrts: Cully scored a couple of tries and beat Breyton Paulse twice in a chase for the ball. Once it was to get his first try and the second time he beat Paulse over 40 metres to save a try.

Cully's one of those guys you really enjoy being near on the field, if you're lucky enough to be near him when he's at full gallop. At that point you're obviously not near him for long.

There's just a 'whoosh' as he goes past. In Christchurch I popped a wee chip kick through and he just launched onto it.

Justin: In general it was a hard old slog, but we ground out what was a pretty good victory against a team who were hard up on defence and tried to shut us down.

Tri-Nations III: August 5

Australia beat the All Blacks 24–23 at the Westpac Trust Stadium, Wellington.

For Australia: Tries by Stirling Mortlock and Joe Roff; three penalty goals and a conversion by Mortlock; penalty goal by John Eales.

For the All Blacks: Two tries by Christian Cullen; three penalty goals and two conversions by Andrew Mehrtens.

Both: They had a very good start, while we got away to a shocker. Daniel Herbert cut through for a Stirling Mortlock try, and then Joe Roff got one too, before we started to claw our way back into the game.

Justin: Right from the start the whole hype surrounding the game was amazing. I remember they kicked off deep and we ran it back at them.

We looked to carry the ball to them, rather than kicking it and allowing them to regain possession.

In that first 15 minutes, while we made some good progress, we eventually turned the ball over and the Australians made us pay for that. But we stuck to our guns with the running game and eventually it started to pay off.

Both: The Christian Cullen try where we moved the ball to the middle of the field from a lineout, then made three switches of direction, was described by Murray Mexted as the best set piece try he'd ever seen the All Blacks score from in a test.

Mehrts: We'd been doing a move that relied on forwards being really eager on getting across to the breakdown, and not leaving anyone blindside in a quick sort of switch across.

When we changed the direction in the midfield in Wellington, it left Jason Little flat-footed, which gave Tana Umaga the slight 'outside' on him, which, with a fend, got Tana clear to feed Cully for the try.

In a variation on the move, I have to get on the outside, get right out of the way, and then follow up and possibly support.

I gave Jonah the flick pass. He gave it to Tana, and then I half turned inside, seeing Tana beating Little, and there was just a rush of air as Cully – the Paekakariki Express – took the pass and went flying through.

I thought, 'There's no way I'm going to get anywhere near him (Cully)'. So I just screamed out, 'Go fellas'. It was bloody good to watch. I often tell people I've got the best seat in the house. That was certainly the case on this occasion.

Justin: The score kept going back and forth and it really was a hell of a game to play in. The feeling in the stadium was electric, just out of this world.

Mehrts and I were both off before the end of the game and I thought we were starting to get on top. But then it turned to custard in the last 10 minutes.

Mehrts: When John Eales stepped up to take a penalty for the win in the last minute of the game, it was just so much like a fairytale; you just knew it was going to happen for him. It was like imagining Jeff Wilson taking his last kick in rugby from the sideline to win a match. You almost had a premonition that he was going to get it.

Oddly enough the kick wasn't that flash. Justin and I were off by then and we had a good view from right behind him. But even if it bent over a bit, it never looked like missing, and that was really the end of the story.

While it was very disappointing at the end, we still had the game with South Africa at Ellis Park to go, and we did take a lot of confidence out of the fact that for large parts of the game we had played the way we wanted to.

Tri-Nations IV August 19

South Africa beat the All Blacks 46–40 at Ellis Park, Johannesburg.

For South Africa: Tries by Robbie Fleck (2), Werner Swanepool (2), Chester Williams and Thinus Delport; two penalty goals and five conversions by Braam van Straaten.

For the All Blacks: Tries by Tana Umaga (2) and Christian Cullen (2); three penalty goals, four conversions and a dropped goal by Andrew Mehrtens.

Both: In a way the test was almost a dead ringer to the game we'd had in the Crusaders earlier in the year against the Cats. They got away to a blinder, we ended up coming back and being on top, and then they ran away again in the end.

Mehrts: The South Africans get bagged for being one-dimensional and relying purely on brute strength. But when you play against them, you know that they're not. **They're big, strong, aggressive guys, but that doesn't mean they haven't got skills.**

Their backs have always had an attacking mindset. For them it's basically about having a go.

Robbie Fleck started the scoring when he went through between me and Pita Alatini. 'Rassie' Erasmus was the third or fourth runner off the ruck, and when I saw a forward running third or fourth off the ruck, I thought he'd have a crack at going over the top of me. Ala did the right thing, he stayed on his man, who was outside Fleck.

I figured I had to stay on Erasmus and when he passed to Fleck I couldn't get close to him.

Justin: The three test matches that we lost in 2000 all saw us get right back into the frame after bad starts, but then fail to keep the momentum going. That was really the story of our season.

The fact we were able to come back on each occasion does show good character, but the fact we couldn't finish off also shows we still have a bit to learn in those situations.

Mehrts: Altitude isn't too much of a factor at Ellis Park now. We're fit enough, you get plenty of water during a game, the bench gets used enough to give players a break, and the adrenaline usually keeps you in it anyway.

I think on the old longer tours it would have been tougher. The tour would have been draining anyway and then when you got up to altitude it knocked you round more.

Ellis Park is a ground I do enjoy playing at, although it's very noisy and the spectators are very aggressive, with a lot of passion. It certainly can see the home team, whether it's the Cats or the Springboks, get a real rush of blood from the energy in the stadium. It gets them really fired up.

I actually like the atmosphere and the ground itself is always in tremendous nick. As a kicker, you obviously find it a lot easier to get distance.

Justin: I made a real blue at the media conference the day after the game. Cully and I had been talking straight after the test about how we hadn't clicked that well and we thought that if we'd got things really going we might have been able to win by 30 points.

I mentioned it at the conference the next day, sort of in jest. We weren't saying we thought we could beat them by 30 points, or that we were 30 points better as team, I was just trying to explain how we felt on the day.

When I phoned home there was a storm over arrogant All Blacks saying they thought they were 30 points better, which wasn't what we meant.

What was hard to explain was why we didn't play to our potential, why sometimes it just doesn't happen. Everyone really tried their best, and we had the Tri-Nations to play for, but it just was one of those games where it didn't come together.

Oops! The Final Hurdle

Canterbury played the first two games of the Air New Zealand NPC in 2000 without most of their All Blacks, who were involved in the Tri-Nations competition.

Game one: August 11

Wellington beat Canterbury 27–20 at Wellington.
For Wellington: Tries by Elvis Seveali'i, Filo Tiatia and Inoke Afeaki; two penalty goals and three conversions by David Holwell.
For Canterbury: Tries by Marika Vunibaka and Ben Hurst; penalty goal and conversion by Ben Blair; penalty goal and conversion by Leon MacDonald.

Game two: August 18

Canterbury beat North Harbour 31–3 at Christchurch.
For Canterbury: Tries by Caleb Ralph, Mark Mayerhofler and Billy Fulton; four penalty goals and two conversions by Ben Blair.
For North Harbour: Penalty goal by Marc Ellis.

Mehrts: It'd be fair to say that in South Africa the All Black doctor, John Mayhew, who's a Harbour man, took a bit of a hiding, along with Troy Flavell and Ron Cribb, over that result.

Doc Mayhew's a good man to rib, because he's always positive Harbour will make the top four. To be fair, he takes it pretty well.

Game three: August 26

Canterbury beat Counties-Manukau 30-16 at Christchurch.
For Canterbury: Tries by Reuben Thorne (2), Derek Maisey and Billy Fulton; two penalty goals and two conversions by Ben Blair.
For Counties-Manukau: Tries by Salesi Moimoi and Joeli Vidiri; two penalty goals by Blair Feeney.

Both: We didn't play in that game, although some of the boys from the All Black squad did. We had a rest until the game at Eden Park.

Game four: September 1

Canterbury beat Auckland 29-26 at Auckland.
For Canterbury: Tries by Justin Marshall (2), Caleb Ralph and Leon MacDonald; penalty goal and two conversions by Andrew Mehrtens; conversion by Ben Blair.
For Auckland: Tries by Steve Devine, Adrian Cashmore and Keven Mealamu; three penalty goals and a conversion by Adrian Cashmore.

Mehrts: It was a big game for Justin. He scored two vital tries in the second half and then he was the one who beat Malili Mauliaina to the ball at the death to save the match.

Justin's always so competitive, pushing himself really hard, so if there's anyone who's the most likely to score a match-winning try, and then get back and save one, then the first pick for most of us in the team would be Justin.

Justin: That chase with Malili turned out to be my downfall. Just before I dived on the ball I took a big stride and my hamstring tightened right up.

I wasn't thinking too much about it at the time, but the hamstring was still a bit tight and sore, and on the training on Tuesday, it actually tore.

Mind you, to beat Auckland up there you'd do the same thing again.

Mehrts: Ben Blair took over the kicking when he came on to replace Leon MacDonald. I'd been pretty muscle sore after the Tri-Nations and I hadn't been able to do a lot of practising. The combination of the soreness and lack of kicking meant that I didn't find any rhythm at Eden Park. I kicked one and missed one, and the one I missed, I missed badly.

So when Ben – who had been kicking very well – came on I was happy for him to take over. If I was 100 per cent I wouldn't automatically expect to be kicking anyway, and to tell the truth it was quite good to be able to get my breath back after someone had scored a try and Ben was taking the conversion.

It was never something that Robbie (Deans) was concerned about, or that Ben was fussed over. Ben was always happy for me to take them, but I always said, 'No, you're kicking so well, go ahead and take them.'

Justin: In my whole career I've only had one easy game with Auckland, in 1998, when we came back from being with the All Blacks and beat them 50–17 at Eden Park.

But apart from that it's always a hell of a battle. Auckland-Canterbury games are always a dogfight. We have respect for each other, which means nobody wants to come out the loser, so we just go at it hammer and tongs.

When I was first in the Canterbury team we suffered some hardships against Auckland and although we've had the wood on them in the last few years, it's never been easy.

Mehrts: People who are old enough to remember the '60s and '70s will know about the great battles in those eras. **If you're under 40, then the 1980s, and in particular the epic Ranfurly Shield game of 1985 when Auckland took the shield, will be a huge memory.**

I know that when I was young I really enjoyed the Ranfurly Shield era of the '80s, and when I was out on the lawn kicking a ball round as a kid, it was always Canterbury playing Auckland in my mind.

So it's a big thrill for me to play against Auckland. They're always a big threat and one of the teams other sides aspire to beat.

It was a very good win to get under our belt because the game was very tight and we had to show some character to get through.

Game five: September 9

Canterbury beat Taranaki 43–9 at New Plymouth.
For Canterbury: Tries by Daryl Gibson (3), Mark Robinson, Afato So'oalo and Norm Maxwell; penalty goal and five conversions by Ben Blair.
For Taranaki: Three penalty goals by Daryl Lilley.

Mehrts: We've had a good recent history in New Plymouth. We know they've got a very tough forward pack and we've got respect for them as a team.

They have a lot of the same values that we tend to identify with in Canterbury, so we know that it's always going to be a battle.

It's easy to get motivated when we go to New Plymouth. We had a very good win in 1998 when we held them tryless, and we did that again in 2000.

(Justin was out for the Taranaki and Southland games with his injured hamstring).

Game six: September 16

Canterbury beat Southland 71–8 at Christchurch.
For Canterbury: Tries by Caleb Ralph (2), Ben Blair (2), Afato So'oalo (2), Reuben Thorne, Marika Vunibaka, Greg Somerville and Daryl Gibson; two penalty goals and six conversions by Ben Blair; penalty goal by Andrew Mehrtens.
For Southland: Try by Anthony Lafaiali'i; penalty goal by David Hill.

Mehrts: Things really clicked against Southland. We'd had about four games with everyone back in the squad and we were probably reaching our peak for the season.

Unfortunately for us in the NPC it was a bit early. There was nothing the coaches could do; it was just a matter of the combinations and confidence among the guys. At that point, other teams were probably still working out how to combat us.

Game seven: September 23

Canterbury beat Waikato 26–18 at Hamilton.
For Canterbury: Tries by Marika Vunibaka and Justin Marshall; four penalty goals and two conversions by Ben Blair.
For Waikato: Tries by Roger Randle and Keith Lowen; two penalty goals and a conversion by Glen Jackson.

Both: In 1998 we'd challenged for the shield in Hamilton and got cleaned out by a team who played bloody well against us.

After we'd lost in '98, we went back up there the following week for the NPC semifinal and they beat us again. So there weren't many recent fond memories of Hamilton. We all knew what we were in for.

Mehrts: We were quite confident in 2000 but, like 1998, we weren't over-confident. We knew that we had to give it a good crack and attack to try to win the shield.

Justin: Waikato had a very good run with the shield and when you go there and play at Rugby Park in Hamilton, they're playing for keeps.

We were quite fortunate that we had quite a few players who had been there in '98 and we knew the passion they'd play with. So we were prepared to try to meet that head on.

Mehrts: The night before the game the wind was exactly the same as it was during the game, which was quite strong. I was getting back into a bit of kicking, mostly to cover if Ben Blair was off the field at any stage.

Ben doesn't like kicking the day before a game, but I quite like to. So we were just wandering around the field and I went over to one side and had a few kicks so we could see which way the wind was going. I ended up landing all of them.

The first shot Ben had in the game was from a similar position. I was back at about halfway, and I was thinking, 'Now, we both saw last night which way the wind was going. I hope you remember it okay'. He just stepped up and drilled it, so he obviously had.

When we got home the schools in Canterbury wanted to get a look at the shield, which is always great to see. There's still a fascination with the shield, even with little kids.

Parents want to get their kids' photos taken with the shield and the reverence that's still there for it is a reflection of the mystique that goes with the shield.

Game eight: September 30

Canterbury beat Otago 29–26 at Christchurch.
For Canterbury: Tries by Marika Vunibaka (2) and Caleb Ralph; four penalty goals and a conversion by Ben Blair.
For Otago: Tries by Hayden Reid, Justin Swart and Byron Kelleher; three penalty goals and a conversion by Tony Brown.

Mehrts: In a way, the Otago challenge was like the 1994 shield game where we were behind, but kept working our way back into a good position on the field.

Justin: We got out of jail that day against Otago. In hindsight we probably shouldn't have won the game. When you're down by 12 points halfway through the second half, then a team should be able to hold on.

They played out of their skins. I haven't seen Otago fired up like that for a long time. They haven't always played at the top of their game in the last couple of seasons, but they were out to do damage in the shield game. It had been a pretty average NPC for them and they wanted to set it right . . . take it out on us.

Mehrts: We were still down four minutes from the end when I made a bit of a break and looked to see who to pop the ball up to.

There was a lineup of Canterbury players looming up. I tried to float it high to the next forward coming up, who I think was Reuben Thorne. Then there was a flash of red and black and Caleb Ralph came flying up and basically intercepted the pass!

He just grabbed it, went racing through, and everyone in

OOPS! THE FINAL HURDLE

the Canterbury team was happy. Caleb's one of those guys who's a pleasure to watch when he's running. He just glides over the ground.

Game nine: October 6

Canterbury beat Northland 28–22 at Christchurch.
For Canterbury: Tries by Justin Marshall (2), Andrew Mehrtens and Mark Mayerhofler; four conversions by Ben Blair.
For Northland: Fero Lasagavibau (2) and Tony Monaghan; penalty goal and two conversions by Hayden Taylor.

Mehrts: We were quite happy that Norm Berryman didn't turn up for the game, but Northland certainly gave it a hell of a nudge.

We expected them to be tough and I don't know so much that we were tired, more that they gave it a good whack. In the first division now every team is capable of pushing any other team hard.

In the end we were very pleased to get home with the win because it meant that the shield stayed in Canterbury for the summer.

Justin: I think we were perhaps a little bit underdone after the Otago game. Northland can be very unpredictable – they certainly were in that game. They played extremely well and gave us a real run for our money.

Semifinal: October 14

Canterbury beat Taranaki 31–23 at Christchurch.
For Canterbury: Tries by Marika Vunibaka, Mark Mayerhofler and Scott Robertson; four penalty goals and two conversions by Ben Blair.
For Taranaki: Tries by Fa'apolou So'olefai and Lome Fa'atau; three penalty goals and two conversions by Daryl Lilley.

Mehrts: I think that Taranaki felt they had nothing to lose when they came to the semifinal. The last couple of times we've played them in New Plymouth they may have felt under a bit of pressure because people were talking up their chances.

171

This time we'd given them a bit of a thumping at the Bullring and they came down and flung everything into it.

Justin: It was a weird sort of game. Nobody was giving Taranaki too much of a chance and the crowd was very small, just 13,000 people.

There had been talk about the amateur team having to play professionals and we knew what the Taranaki boys felt about it, so we were prepared to meet fire with fire.

They were bloody tough, and it wasn't just up front, either. Their backs played really well, too. I think they'd learnt a hell of a lot from the game in the round robin and they seemed to go into the semi with a really strict game plan, which they stuck to.

They just kept banging away at their game plan and I don't think we ever got real ascendancy at any stage in the match. **We went through some good patches, but really we just managed to get points at the right time.**

Mehrts: Against Taranaki, Sam Broomhall, our No 8, had another very good game. Sam's bigger than he looks. I'm sometimes surprised standing alongside him, because when you see him on TV he doesn't look as big as he really is.

He's very tough and in some ways is quite deceptive. He possibly is one of the guys that people have underestimated. He certainly sat a few guys on their butts in 2000.

Sam's a good keen man, very willing, quite humble, a guy who cut his teeth on country rugby in North Canterbury. His old man looks like 'Grizz' Wyllie, which is a good thing, too. I thought that was ideal.

Final: October 21

Wellington beat Canterbury 34–29 at Christchurch.
For Wellington: Tries by Jonah Lomu (2), Inoke Afeaki and Jason O'Halloran; two penalty goals and four conversions by David Holwell.
For Canterbury: Tries by Andrew Mehrtens and Todd Blackadder; four penalty goals and two conversions by Ben Blair; penalty goal by Andrew Mehrtens.

Both: It was a game where we knew we were in for a hell of a time because they'd beaten us in the round robin and the Hurricanes had beaten us in Super 12.

They got away to a very good start, with a try from a set move to Jonah, after Jason O'Halloran put through a little grubber kick, and then Cully got a good try, too.

Justin: For 60 minutes of the game they dominated us before we made a comeback. With 15 minutes to go we were down 34–15, so to get close took a huge effort.

Mehrts: It was a disappointing end for Canterbury, but I think most people throughout the country agreed that the way Wellington played in the last three or four weeks of the NPC they certainly deserved it.

We had to hand it to them. They may not have been the most consistent team in the NPC, but that doesn't matter. The Crusaders haven't been the most consistent team in Super 12, but produced it when it mattered, and Wellington certainly produced it when it mattered in the NPC.

From the Canterbury end, we felt we'd given it a big effort, but we didn't have any argument with Wellington winning it.

It was an odd one when Toddy was injured scoring his try at the end. There's some suggestion his face may have smacked into his own hand when he slammed the ball down.

If that was the case, it'd be typical Blackadder, because it doesn't matter where you hit him, it's painful.

He may have the biggest butt in the team – and the All Blacks as well – and you'd think there'd be a bit of cushioning there. But no matter where you tackle him, high, low, or anywhere, you strike bone . . . and it hurts.

If he did cop some of his own medicine then perhaps his face is the softest point, which may be a hint to where you should tackle him.

You're Nicked – And Named

Dave Abercrombie – *Abo*
Pita Alatini – *Ala* or *Mr Bliss*
Norm Berryman – *Normie*
Todd Blackadder – *Toddy*
Andrew Blowers – *AB*
Mike Brewer – *Bruiser*
Robin Brooke – *Bully*
Zinzan Brooke – *Zinny* or *Easter Island*
Tony Brown – *Brownie* or *Dummy*
Ron Cribb – *Cribby*
Christian Cullen – *Cully* or *Crowbar* or *Bar* or *C. Bar*
Sean Fitzpatrick – *Fitzy*
Troy Flavell – *Flavs*
Richard Fry – *Ravishing Rick* or *Frybee* or *Stir Fry* . . . and
    endless other 'Fry' derivations
Daryl Gibson – *Gibbo* or *Leonard* or *Lenny*
Tony Gilbert – *Big Tee* or *Medium Tee*
Mark Hammett – *Hammer*
John Hart – *Harty*
Carl Hoeft – *Bulldog*
Gordon Hunter – *Gordie*
Alama Ieremia – *Milan*
Ian Jones – *Kamo*

Byron Kelleher – *Wozzer*
Josh Kronfeld – *Crusher* or *Russia* or *Crunch*
  or *Lunch* or *Flush*
Jonah Lomu – *Big Guy* or *Da Bomb*
Leon MacDonald – *Rangi*
Justin Marshall – *Marshy*
Andrew Martin – *The Colonel* (never, ever *Andy*)
Norm Maxwell – *Big Boy* or *Taxi* or *Maxi Taxi*
Mark Mayerhofler – *Bubs*
John Mayhew – *Hewie*
Colin Meads – *Pinetree* or *Tree*
Andrew Mehrtens – *Mehrts* or *Don't Cut Your Hair*
Kees Meuws – *Bad News Meuws* or *Sunday Meuws*
  or *One Network Meuws* etc . . .
Anton Oliver – *Hatchet* or *Two Bottles*
Glen Osborne – *Oz*
Taine Randell – *Teapot*
Bruce Reihana – *Bruiser*
Scott Robertson – *Razor* or *François*
Mark Robinson – *Robbo*
Dallas Seymour – *Tom Thumb*
Peter Sloane – *Sloaney*
Wayne Smith – *Smithy* or *Mahoney*
Carlos Spencer – *Los*
Tana Umaga – *Glenn McGrath*
Royce Willis – *The Whopper*
Jeff Wilson – *Goldie*